LAMPS

Souvenir Press Collector's Guide Series
Mugs and Tankards by Deborah Stratton
Jugs by James Paton
Buttons by Victor Houart
Easter Eggs by Victor Houart

LAMPS

A Collector's Guide

by
James Paton

SOUVENIR PRESS

CONTENTS

To Pauline, my wife, who has
helped more than she knows

ACKNOWLEDGEMENTS

My thanks for help and advice go firstly to my friend Fred Penny, lamp collector extraordinary. There are many others who have also given encouragement and assistance, among them: Gwen Hughes, George and Grace Oakley, Des and Marguerite Dwyer, Peter Johnson, Joan and Fred Crickard, Barry Gordon, Derrick Norman and Christopher Wray.

DEFEAT OF THE DARK

'. . . but what am I?
An infant crying in the night;
An infant crying for the light.'

Thus it has always been. Darkness is the enemy, concealing dangers, menacing, reminding us all of the closeness of death. But light is life . . . .

So for more than 30,000 years men have sought ways to lighten the darkness that surrounds them for half their lives.

For the very earliest caveman the only source of illumination was the flickering, smouldering fire around which he and his fellows crouched at night. And the first portable light, the forerunner of the lamp, was the blazing piece of wood plucked from the fire, perhaps to be used for protection against some marauding animal or to investigate those unnerving, sleep-preventing sounds that always seem to emanate from distant dark corners and crannies.

The discovery of the torch in this way should, in all logic, have meant that the fire itself would no longer be used as a principal source of light. The torch could easily be wedged into a fissure in the cave wall—the first wall lamp— or stuck into a piece of clay to support it. Yet long after rushlights, candles and even lamps had been developed, the fire continued to be used for lighting. In medieval Europe fire baskets or 'cressets' were carried on poles or set up on raised platforms to give light out of doors. Old prints show that the cresset, or fire basket, on a pole was still being used by the old watch bands in England in the eighteenth century,. The firebasket was also the first lighthouse, set up on shores and wharves to guide seamen. It was probably in use centuries before the Christian era by the Greeks and Phoenicians. The Greek word *pharos* (a beacon) is derived from the name of the first lighthouse, the Pharos of Alexandria, one of the wonders of the ancient world. The light of its fires was said to be visible as far as 40 miles away and it remained in existence until it was destroyed by earthquake in the thirteenth century. The Romans built lighthouses or pharos' throughout their empire, including one at Dover and another on the other side of the English Channel at Boulogne. Fires continued to be used as lighthouse beacons, fuelled first with wood and then with coal, until the nineteenth century.

The burning torch, too, lit many paths for many centuries, and naturally men found that certain woods burnt better and gave a brighter light than others. Sir Walter Scott in *The Legend of Montrose* gives this description of a torchlit Scottish feast:

Behind every seat stood a gigantic highlander, completely dressed and armed after the fashion of his country, holding in his right hand his drawn sword with the point turned downwards and in the left a blazing torch made of the bog pine. This wood, found in the morasses, is so full of turpentine that, when split and dried, it is frequently used in the highlands instead of candles.

Rushlight holder, English, probably 18th century.
Collection: F. Penny

Even today the torch has its place in ritual and ceremony: one night in the summer of 1977 my wife and I joined the villagers of Taplow in Buckinghamshire as they walked in procession bearing torches up the hillside to light the great bonfire, one of many hundreds of beacon fires that burned on British hillsides to signal the Silver Jubilee of Queen Elizabeth II.

The discovery that certain materials—such as the highlanders' bog pine full of turpentine—burned more readily and reliably than others led to the appearance of the first primitive lamps, which simply consisted of the bodies of oily animals and fish. Even until the early years of this century the Indians on Vancouver Island made use of the small dead fish of the salmon family that were cast up on the shore in vast quantities. All they had to do was stick a strip of fibrous

Left: A fine bronze torch-holder in the shape of a satyr holding a horn shaped torch. Wooden base. Made in Padua, Northern Italy, early 16th century.

Right: Bronze lamp in the shape of a negro head. The projecting lower lip forms the spout. Paduan, 16th century. *Photos: Christies, London*

bark into the mouth of the fish, and when the bark had become impregnated with fish oil, light up. The fish lamp could be held in a cleft stick stuck into the sand. The people of the Scottish Orkney and Shetland islands also found their lamps on the beach. They picked up dead stormy petrels and pushed some kind of wick down through the birds' beaks into their stomachs, which acted as efficient reservoirs of oil from the fish they had consumed. Then they would stick the birds' feet into lumps of clay and they had quite serviceable lamps.

Once again, all they had to do was light up. All, did I say? It wasn't that simple. Modern man in his city apartment unthinkingly

Left: Double oil lamp with a boat-shaped container cast in relief with acanthus foliage, supported by a statue of Judith holding the head of Holdofernes. Paduan, 16th century.

Right: This unusual Roman lamp is moulded in the shape of a sandalled foot. *Photo: Christies, London*

lights his candles or standby oil lamps with safety match or cigarette lighter, when the occasional power cut or failure reminds him that our kind of civilisation may not be permanent after all. But he might reflect for a moment on the problems of his ancestors when the lights went out. It was only in 1826 that John Walker, a chemist from Stockton on Tees in England, invented his "friction lights", the forerunners of the modern match. James Boswell, diarist of Dr Samuel Johnson, described his own predicament when caught in the dark unexpectedly:

> I determined to sit up all night, which I accordingly did and wrote a great deal. About two o'clock in the morning, I inadvertently snuffed out my candle, and as my fire before that was long before black and cold, I was in a great dilemma how to proceed.

12

Downstairs did I softly and silently step to the kitchen. But, alas, there was as little fire there as upon the icy mountains of Greenland. With a tinder box is a light struck every morning to kindle the fire, which is put out at night. I was also apprehensive that my landlord, who always keeps a pair of loaded pistols by him, might fire at me as a thief. I went up to my room, sat quietly until I heard the watchman calling 'past three o'clock'. I then called him to knock at the door of the house where I lodged. He did so, and I opened to him, and got my candle re-lumed without danger.

Even if Boswell had been able to find the tinder box he would probably have had great difficulty in getting a light without grazing his knuckles and being forced to utter a few oaths first.

But some lucky primitive people were able to avoid the problems involved in getting a spark from a tinder box or from two pieces of wood. In South America the Spanish invaders found that the natives made use of great luminous beetles as lamps—two were said to be enough to light a room. And in the West Indies and Japan, where fireflies proliferate, the inhabitants would catch the glowing creatures and imprison them in wooden cages to form lanterns.

Animals and birds were often used as decoration on relief-moulded Roman lamps. The head of a god appears on this Roman pottery lamp. *Photo: Christies, London*

Lamps to light an orgy? The corrupt Emperor Caligula would have approved of these. *Photo: Christies, London*

LIGHT FROM LIFE

~~~~~~

From using lamps made from the bodies of dead fish and stormy petrels it is an obvious step to start extracting oil from fish and animals to use for lighting. But first a container had to be found to hold the oil, and naturally our remote ancestors made use of whatever readily available material was suitable. Pacific islanders probably used coconut shells, as some still do today. People who lived near beaches, on the Mediterranean, for example, or on islands, used shells. Elsewhere, particularly in Northern Europe, hollowed-out stones provided the well or reservoir to hold the animal fat or fish oil.

Archaeologists believe that the first manufactured oil lamps were in fact made of stone. Some of these hollowed-out stones have been found in the caves at Lascaux, France, and have been dated to some 15,000 years ago. There have also been suggestions that other hollowed-out stones known to be 30,000 years old were used as lamps.

It is more difficult to establish when the first shell lamps were made, although it is claimed that they were in existence more than 6,000 years ago. Old shells, even if the natural orifices have been enlarged, apparently to create a channel for the wick, are difficult to identify positively as lamps. It is believed, however, that shell-shaped lamps made of alabaster dug up with Sumerian remains of about 2600 BC were copies of real shell lamps that had been in use in the area for many centuries.

The shells most often used for oil lamps, because of their size and shape, were oyster and whelk shells, and in the Orkneys and Shetlands a popular form of lamp was the *buckie* lamp, suspended by a cord from the roof. It was made from the shell of the 'buckie', which was the local name for the red whelk.

The prevalence of shell lamps in the Mediterranean area is

confirmed by the large number of shell-shaped pottery lamps that
have been found there by archaeologists, many of them copies of the
scallop shell. In addition to those made of pottery and stone, shell
lamps have been found made of bronze and lead also.

Early copies of stone lamps in pottery and bronze, however, are not
easily identifiable. Stone lamps have continued to be used in
Scandinavia and Alaska until quite recent times. The Eskimos in
Alaska used hollowed-out soapstone lamps which were often used
for cooking and heating as well as for lighting. They had wicks of
powdered moss laid along one edge, and the fuel was whale or seal
blubber. Stone lamps with human figures carved in the centre of the
bowls have been found in excavations of a prehistoric settlement in
Greenland.

The ancient Egyptians, like the Sumerians, are known to have
used lamps made of stone, although the very early lamps were
probably shells. It is a curious fact that very few lamps have been
discovered among Egyptian relics, although from ancient writings it
is known that they were widely used. Herodotus mentions a festival
of lamps at which the people of Sais burned hundreds of lamps in the
open outside their homes. These lamps were shaped like saucers in
which a wick floated on top of a mixture of castor oil and salt. Most
early Egyptian lamps are believed to have been saucer shaped, and
this may account for the fact that so few old lamps have been

16

identified: a simple saucer, lacking a spout or a lip blackened at the edge from a burning wick, would not be easy to recognise as a lamp. One beautiful example made of alabaster found in Tutankhamen's tomb in the 1920s was at first thought to be a drinking cup. In fact it is a triple lamp in the shape of three lotus flowers. The central lotus is wide open and the two smaller lamps at each side represent the flower in bud. Other alabaster lamps found in the tomb were at first thought to be vases: they were positively identified as lamps when a light placed in one of the vases revealed a colour picture that was visible only when it was illuminated from the inside. The 'vase' had a double bowl, with a hidden picture on the surface of the inner bowl.

Three typical Roman pottery oil lamps with low relief decoration. *Photo: Christies, London*

A fine Roman pottery standing lamp. *Photo: Christies, London*

An attractive float-wick glass lamp, probably 18th century. The wick might have been supported by a cork. This kind of lamp is sometimes mistakenly described as a lacemaker's lamp. *Photo: Phillips*

In ancient China, too, the open saucer lamp was the normal form of illumination. The Chinese lamps were often supported on elaborate stands of bronze, pewter or iron made in the shape of birds or animals. Sometimes they were adapted as hanging lamps.

By the time of the Roman occupation of Egypt, the simple saucer lamp had developed a spout to carry the wick. In fact spouted saucer lamps became the norm throughout the near and Middle East, made of pottery, bronze or brass. These spouted saucer lamps eventually acquired a foot and curved handle, and so developed into the type of magic lamp that Aladdin rubs on stage every Christmas to produce his friendly genie.

The early Greek lamps, about 600 BC, were apparently copies of the Egyptian spouted saucer lamps. (It was the Greeks who gave us the English word *lamp*, from *lampas*—a light). They soon improved on the basic Egyptian lamp, turning the rim inwards so that there was less chance of the oil spilling. Then they put a bridge over the nozzle to hold the wick securely. Most ancient Greek lamps were turned on the potter's wheel and usually lack any decoration, although they are often glazed. A feature that distinguishes some of these Greek lamps from similar Roman ones is that the nozzle was often spoon-shaped. These lamps were made in enormous numbers, as were similar Parthian lamps. The Parthian lamps had long downward pointing nozzles and burned sesame oil; the Greeks used olive oil. Many Greek and Roman lamps were multi-spouted, some made to hang from ceilings, others to be placed on a plinth, which was often adjustable. One lamp found in the buried city of Pompeii had 14 spouts. And one shop in Herculaneum had a huge, multi-spouted bronze lamp hanging from the ceiling.

The many lamps found in the excavations of these two cities demonstrated how much lavish detail and craftsmanship the Romans employed when they made their lamps. Many they made in the shapes of animals—lions, bear, deer, horses, eagles, goats, dogs, rabbits and so on. On others they carved relief designs depicting gods, goddesses, gladiators and mythological subjects. One fine lamp at Herculaneum represents the jolly god Silenus with an owl sitting on his head between two huge horns, each of which supports a lampstand. Another represents a flower stalk growing out of a circular plinth, with snail shells hanging from it by small chains, each shell holding oil and a wick. Yet another is a figure of a naked boy with a lamp hanging from one hand and an instrument for trimming the wick from the other, the lamp itself representing a theatrical mask. Beside him is a twisted column surmounted by the head of a faun which has a lid in its crown and seems to be intended as a reservoir for oil. The boy and pillar are both placed on a square plateau raised on lions' claws. One is struck by the tremendous display of elaborate craftsmanship in return for what must have been quite feeble illumination!

But in addition to these splendid showpieces the Romans produced vast quantities of simple pottery and lead lamps, and it was these that made some sort of night life possible for the high-living citizens. That callous and wicked Emperor Caligula, lover of orgies and debauchery, had actors perform in front of him by the light of hundreds of ordinary Roman lamps. Domitian, too, liked to be entertained during the long hours of the night, but he preferred to watch gladiators fight for their lives by lamplight.

The main difference between the everyday pottery Roman lamp and its Greek equivalent was that the Roman utensil was almost completely closed in, the top forming a shallow depressed bowl with one or two filling holes which would contain wooden plugs when the lamp was in use. The depression made it possible to fill the lamp through these small holes without spilling the oil. The bowl was also often decorated with animal figures, flowers or scenes of gladiatorial combat in relief.

Some rather fanciful lamps were made by the Romans in the shapes of animals, or objects such as the human head or foot. Usually these lamps have ring handles for carrying.

Many Roman lamps were designed specifically for use in religious ceremonies. In all civilisations the temples and places of worship have had their own special forms of lighting. The Hebrews, for example, had the seven-branched candlestick with its own religious significance. The term candlestick, although it appears in the Old Testament, is in fact a misnomer, for the apparatus was in fact a group of float-wick lamps. In *Exodus* the Jews are instructed:

Thou shalt make a candlestick of pure gold: of beaten work shall the candlestick be made; his shaft and his branches, his bowls, his knobs and his flowers shall be of the same. And six branches shall

come out of the sides of it; three branches of the candlestick out of one side, and three branches of the candlestick out the other side. Three bowls made like unto almonds, with a knop and a flower in one branch; and three bowls made like unto almonds in the other branch, with a knop and a flower: so in the six branches that come out of the candlestick. And in the candlestick shall be four bowls made like unto almonds, with their knops and their flowers. And there shall be a knop under two branches of the same, and a knop under two branches of the same, and a knop under two branches of the same, according to the six branches that proceed out of the candlestick. Their knops and their branches shall be of the same: all of it shall be one beaten work of pure gold. And thou shalt make the seven lamps thereof; and they shall light the lamps thereof, that they may give light over against it. And the tongs thereof, and the snuff dishes thereof, shall be of pure gold. Of a talent of pure gold shall he make it, with all these vessels. And look that thou make them after their pattern, which was shewed thee in the mount.

Later there are several references to oil for the lamp. For example: And thou shalt command the children of Israel, that they bring thee pure oil-olive beaten for the light, to cause the lamp to burn always.

The seven-branch 'candlestick' was followed by the Hanukkah lamp, which has not seven, but eight different spouted oil lamps and

Two beautiful blue and white pottery lamps by Wedgwood in the Roman style. Late 18th century. Photo: Christies, London

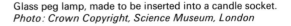

commemorates the rededication of the temple by Judas Maccabaeus in 165 BC, after the Syrians had desecrated it and used it as a pagan altar. It was necessary to relight the perpetual light of the temple and it was discovered that there was only one flask of oil left, enough for one day. But by a miracle the oil in the flask lasted for eight days. Nowadays the Hanukkah lamp is lit, one lamp each day, throughout the eight days of the festival.

Some Indian temple lamps are similar to the Hanukkah lamp in that they have several reservoirs. These are usually in the shape of a brass female figure holding before her a number of spoon-shaped reservoirs with a pilot light above. In one version the female goddess is seated on an elephant, the lamp bowls in front of her, and the pilot light in the elephant's trunk. Simpler versions have the luck-bringing goddess holding a single spoon-shaped reservoir. It was the custom for the worshipper to purchase a spoonful of oil so that the flame could be kept burning while he prayed—in the same way that candles are available for sale in Catholic churches.

There are also multiple lamps without the figure of the goddess, but with a cobra-head handle. Other Indian lamps made of brass have a deep body like a vase, which holds oil from which the lamp bowl can be refilled. This bowl is usually a round shallow trough around the top of the vase with a channel for the wick. The vase section has a snake handle with several cobra heads which overshadow a small figure of a deity.

In Ceylon there were gravity-fed lamps with reservoirs shaped like a bird with a hollow body, from which the lamp bowl at its feet is kept full. These bird lamps were usually suspended from the ceiling. Another interesting type was the lotus lamp with separate brass or copper petals. When the lamp was not in use it was shaped like a closed lotus bud, but when this was unscrewed a round bowl to hold the oil, shaped like the centre of an open lotus blossom, was revealed.

Other old temple lamps were of the floating wick variety, descending from the Egyptian saucer lamp, which is represented in many ancient tomb paintings as a bowl containing a flame. In these lamps there was never any groove or spout for the wick, which merely floated on the surface of the oil in the lamp, perhaps supported by a small raft of cork or other lightweight substance. This was the type of lamp adopted by the early Christian Church, and also by the Muslims after their conquest of Egypt. Religious men in the Christian monastic orders took this type of lamp with them into the European monasteries, while the Moors spread its use across their empire throughout North Africa and Spain. The earliest kinds were either simple bowls or cones, with the pointed end at the base, and were mainly employed as hanging lamps, although some also had handles so that they could be carried. The traditional and distinctive mosque lamp with its bell-shaped top from which a number of glass cylinders are suspended employs the float-wick principle. Each of the glass cylinders is a separate lamp with the wick floating on the oil. The oil itself is usually floating on water, so that the flame always appears to be high up in the glass cylinders for better diffusion of the light. It was a common device to float the oil in water in float-wick lamps made of glass.

Float-wick lamps remained common in European monasteries until the Middle Ages; and in eastern mosques, synagogues and palaces well into the twentieth century. Like many other types of oil lamp, many of them have now been converted for use as electric lamps. Decoration on eastern float-wick lamps was often lavish and there was some especially fine enamelling on glass lamps of the fourteenth century. The lamp-holders or containers were often elaborate metal structures. In Jewish homes the lamp normally used was a simple bowl with a float, perhaps for several wicks, which was lit every Friday.

But surely all these ancient lamps, you might think, are beyond the dreams of the ordinary collector. Happily, and particularly in the case of Roman lamps, this need not be so. Pottery and metal lamps were made in immense quantities for use throughout the Roman Empire, and large numbers have survived. It is possible to buy an old Roman lamp for a small fraction of the cost of some of the twentieth-century electric lamps of the Art Nouveau and Art Deco periods.

For many people, to be able to own and handle pieces of such antiquity is supremely satisfying. And it doesn't cost a fortune.

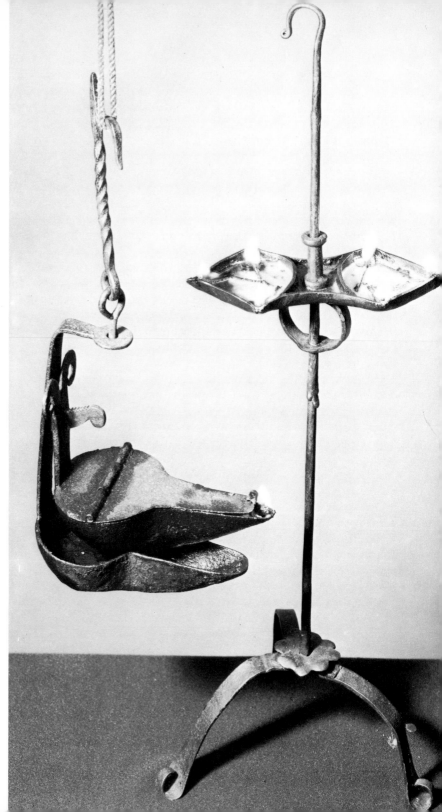

The Scottish crusie
iron lamp, with drip
pan, and an adjustable
iron pan lamp, made in
Switzerland. Lamps
like these were used
for centuries. These are
probably 19th century.
*Photo: Lent to the
Science Museum,
London, by the
Gaslight and Coke Co.*

THE SPARK OF SUPERSTITION

~~~~~~

In the flickering, always feeble light of early oil lamps it was easy for the imagination to evoke another world of ghosts and demons that seemed to populate the darkness outside. And in the superstitious Celtic areas of northern Europe, where the same type of primitive lamp was in use from the Iron Age right through until the early years of twentieth century, there were many weird beliefs connected with the dancing, always on the point of disappearing, flame. If it burnt with a blue tinge, according to the people of the Channel Islands, there would be a wind next day. A green flame signified that there were witches close by—and no doubt many an unexpected caller at a humble shack was viewed with suspicion if he or she arrived when the flame of the lamp had given this warning. A sudden spark flying towards you, however, had no sinister meaning. It indicated that there was news on the way for you.

The long-lived lamp around which the fey Celts sat for generation after generation, spinning their weird tales of the spirit world and passing on such superstitions, is generally known as the *crusie*, the name given to it by the Scots. In America, where it was introduced by European settlers, it was given feminine names—sometimes the Betty lamp and sometimes the Phoebe lamp.

The crusie has a pear-shaped or oval iron bowl attached to a long handle, which curves back over the bowl and hooks on to a spike which can be driven into a wall. Alternatively the crusie can be suspended by a hook from the ceiling. Many crusies have a double bowl, the lower bowl being a safety measure and also perhaps, an economy measure, being there to catch any drips from the main bowl containing the oil. The upper reservoir bowl also has a toothed rack arrangement so that it can be tilted gradually as the level of the oil gets low—another example of Scottish thrift. The most sophisticated version of the crusie has a hinged lid for the main bowl.

Primitive pottery open-stand lamp of indeterminate age. Lamps like this were in use from Saxon times until about 1850. *Collection: Author*

Because iron is subject to corrosion, no very early iron crusies exist, the oldest probably being about 200 years old.

Similar iron lamps were used in many parts of Europe, usually of the single bowl type, and it is thought that the first of these lamps in use in the United States were taken there by Germans who settled in Pennsylvania.

Another type of iron lamp in use throughout Europe was the simple pan lamp. One Swiss version has two flat pans with a rim, which can be raised or lowered along a central pillar to adjust the height. Unlike the crusie, which has only one wick outlet, this pan lamp has six wicks, three to each pan, each providing its own flame. This type of European pan lamp was occasionally made in copper or brass (a few examples of crusie-type lamps made of brass have also been found in France). Italian examples usually have single pans and are often decorated with incised ornamentation. In Germany, Austria and Switzerland some imagination was used in the design,

Brass reading lamp in the Venetian style. Adjustable. Probably Dutch, 18th century. *Photo: Crown Copyright, Science Museum, London*

Left: A fine bronze lamp, with the Three Graces forming the base. Early 19th century.

Right: Magnificent desk lamp in bronze, probably made for a Paduan palace in the 16th century. The satyr holds the globe of heaven cast with the sun and stars. There is also an inkwell. *Photo: Christies, London*

with the bowls sometimes being square, or heart or clover-leaf shaped. In Norway in the sixteenth century primitive lamps with large iron pans with spouts at the four corners, and covered with smoke shields, were used. These burned cod liver oil.

28

Another primitive lamp which survived in Europe for many centuries was the open stand lamp, usually made of pottery or more rarely of metal. Basically the open stand lamp is a simple bowl or saucer lamp on a candlestick-like base, and usually with a handle. Most of them have a wide base with an upturned rim, to catch any drips, and often this drip basin has a lip so that the rescued oil can be poured into a container for re-use. Italian examples of the open stand lamp often have the pedestal section in the form of a human figure.

A more sophisticated form of European lamp, usually made in durable brass, was the spout lamp. The top was completely enclosed, the wick passed through a long spout and there was a carrying handle: the whole in fact rather like a teapot in shape. The spout lamps often had a pedestal stand and frequently were fitted with a strap at the back so that they could be suspended from a hook. Some were double spouted. Other materials used in their manufacture were pewter, tin and pottery.

The best known of these spout lamps is probably the *lucerna* of Italy. This has a central stem passing through the the centre of the reservoir, so that the height can be adjusted, and has a loop handle at the top of this stem to make it easy to carry. A few spout lamps found in Holland and Belgium have a curved, upturned spout with a collar at the end to catch drips. But most Dutch and Belgian spout lamps are of coffee-pot shape with an inner reservoir fitting inside an outer cylinder. The reservoir has a spout which projects over a drip channel attached to the outer cylinder. Most of them have a pedestal stand with a semi-circular base, so that they can stand close to a wall. The base is either weighted with sand to prevent the lamp from toppling over, or inserted into a wooden block. These lamps are usually made of brass and are often elaborately decorated. They were used first with whale oil and later with colza oil, and date to the eighteenth and nineteenth centuries.

One variation of the Italian *lucerna*, used in both southern Europe and in Holland—perhaps introduced during the Spanish occupation of the Netherlands—was an attractive brass reading lamp, which was adjustable up and down the central brass column. It had three flame spouts and a brass screen to prevent glare. The angle of this glare screen could be adjusted to get the best possible illumination on the pages.

A pair of bronze and ormolu urn-shaped oil lamps in the manner of Thomas Hope. The ebonised stands have gilt metal and gesso embellishment; 40 inches high. Circa 1780. *Photo: Phillips, London*

Up until the eighteenth century, the great majority of European lamps had spouts or wicks protruding at the side. They were convenient to use and were sturdy and, being fully enclosed, fairly safe. But the central wick lamp had obvious advantages, especially as a standing lamp, and it is difficult to understand why the central wick did not come into widespread use until the eighteenth century. Among the earliest English lamps with a central burner were those glass pedestal lamps frequently and incorrectly described as lacemakers' lamps. An upright tube contained the burner, which was inserted into the open top of the bowl in a cork or in a threaded collar made of pewter. These very attractive glass lamps were a development of the earlier glass float-wick lamps, but it is very unusual now to find any of them complete with their original burners.

A Venetian bronze sliding oil lamp. The moving body has two eagle-headed flame spouts. 18th century. *Photo: Bonhams, London*

The central burner lamp became more popular in the United States than in Europe, and it was Benjamin Franklin who first fitted such a lamp with a double burner, considerably increasing the amount of light supplied. There were also experiments with triple burner lamps of this type, but they did not increase the illumination significantly. Most American lamps of the central wick type were made to burn whale oil, which, for lighting, was inferior only to the very best seed oils. There was a plentiful supply of whale oil from the end of the eighteenth century from the flourishing whaling industry which fished the waters of the Pacific and the Bering Straits, but when the price of whale oil started to increase, lard became a more popular fuel. Attempts to find a more efficient fuel led to the introduction of camphene in about 1830. This was in quite widespread use for about 20 years, and special lamps were designed to burn it. These usually have double burners and special caps— rather like candle snuffers—which were put in place over the wicks when the lamps were not in use. The caps were necessary to prevent the evaporation of the camphene, a highly volatile mixture of turpentine and alcohol which proved to be a dangerous explosive fuel. It caused a number of disastrous fires and loss of life before the paraffin lamp ousted all other competitors. Benzene, discovered in 1825, was also used as a lamp fuel.

Another fuel which gave brilliant illumination, and was particularly useful out of doors to illuminate a large area, was naphtha, which is distilled from coal. There were naphtha lamps even in the seventeenth century, and the great English poet John Milton wrote that they "with naphtha and asphaltum yielded light, as from a sky." A new type of naphtha lamp, the Holliday lamp, was developed in the mid-nineteenth century, and continued to be used at outdoor street markets for about 100 years. The burner was wickless and the fuel supply controlled by a needle valve. The oil was vaporised through the heat of the flame and burned through small orifices in a rose burner. To start the lamp from cold it was necessary first to heat it by burning methylated spirit.

Two simple lamps of a type much used in the United States about 1840. The single wick lamp was for burning whale oil. The two-wick lamp burned volatile camphene— for which snuffing caps were essential. *Photo: Crown Copyright, Science Museum, London*

BREAKTHROUGH TO
BRIGHTNESS

~~~~~~

Until the 1780s all oil lamps gave only feeble illumination, and in addition created a lot of smoke and nasty smells—especially when fish oil was the fuel. Well-off people in the eighteenth century who took a pride in their homes suspended large bell-shaped glass smoke-catchers over their lamps to protect their ceilings from becoming smutty and sooty. These smoke bells are very elegant items and are worth collecting for themselves, although because of their fragile nature they have become very scarce.

Until the late eighteenth century, there had in fact been remarkably little change in the oil lamp since Roman times. A simple, soft round cord continued to be used as a wick—it could not be too thick or the cord would not burn in the centre and more smouldering and smoke would be caused. And glass chimneys were not yet employed, although Leonardo da Vinci had effectively demonstrated the value of a draught to increase the power of a flame hundreds of years earlier.

The first notable improvements to increase light-giving qualities came from France. First a Monsieur Leger made the first flat wick of woven cotton—the same kind of wick that is still used in small oil lamps to the present day. Then came a much more important breakthrough. Amie Argand, a scientist from Geneva who was at the time working in Paris, experimented with this flat wick and shaped it into a cylindrical one and placed it between two metal tubes. Through the inner tube a current of air was allowed to pass to the inside of the flame, increasing its brightness. Nevertheless Argand was disappointed with the amount of light obtained, until his partner Quinquet, a French chemist, held the neck of a broken glass bottle over the wick. The increased brilliance was quite dramatic—and the glass chimney was created.

Argand's lamp, which was patented in 1783, was such a vast

improvement on previous lamps that not only did anyone who could afford to do so buy the new lamps for his home, but craftsmen who performed delicate types of work which previously had been restricted to daylight, now found themselves able to work at night. The new lamp gave 12 times as much light from a single wick as any earlier lamp had done.

It was found, however, that the flame of the Argand lamp varied as the level of the oil in the reservoir changed: although the colza oil it burned gave a good light, this was heavy and sticky and did not really soak its way up the wick as fast as it could be burned. By using a form of lamp based on the principle of the bird fountain, placing the reservoir higher up the lamp than the wick, this problem was overcome, but a new one created. Inconvenient shadows were thrown by the reservoir, and the lamps tended to be top-heavy. To avoid this, an alternative to the bird-fountain feed was introduced by Carcel, who invented a clockwork pump for raising the fuel in 1800.

Properly managed, the clockwork pump lamps gave a steady and bright light for seven to eight hours. Unfortunately they were costly to run, using up oil at a great rate, and the mechanism was easily disturbed. An improvement on the Carcel lamp, and one which soon superseded it, was the Moderator, patented in 1835, by Franchot. The oil was stored in the body or pillar of the lamp, and forced up to the wick by means of the pressure of a strong spiral spring on a leather piston. The spring was wound up by a rack and pinion, and the flow was regulated by a tapering rod in the ascending tube, called the 'moderator'. Surplus oil flowed back to the top of the piston.

Many other variations of the Argand lamp were produced during the nineteenth century, a notable example being the Diacon lamp, patented in the United States about 1840, in which a clockwork motor in the base pumped oil through a tube from the reservoir to the wick, rather like the earlier Carcel lamp. Clockwork was also used in the American Hitchcock lamp, invented in 1868. This was a flat-wick kerosene lamp in which the clockwork drove a fan to force air into the flame.

Right: Attractive double student's lamp with cut glass oil reservoirs. Late 19th century. *Collection: F. Penny*

34

Not everyone liked these mechanical devices and many people continued to use lamps with the bird-fountain reservoir. In these the reservoir was filled up with oil until a float valve closed the filling hole, and a cap was screwed into the filling hole so that it was airtight. There was a lower compartment to the reservoir, from which the wick was fed and which had an air intake. This lower compartment was closed by a second float valve, until sufficient oil had burnt or leaked away to open the valve slightly. A little air would then flow into the reservoir and an equal amount of oil flow from the top compartment of the reservoir, raising the level below so that it was closed again by the lower valve. Oil could not drop from the upper reservoir unless air could replace it.

The most popular lamp with this bird-fountain reservoir arrangement was without any shadow of doubt the colza oil Student lamp, with the oil reservoir on one side of a central brass pillar, counterbalanced by the lamp and shade on the other side. The design is so elegant that it was retained even for paraffin lamps, and is widely used for electric lamps today.

The central draught burner used in these Argand lamps had spreaders or air diffusers fitted into the central tube to provide air to the wick, and they will not operate if these are missing. Collectors who want to use their oil lamps with central burners, and find that a lot of smoke is being thrown out or the flame is weak, should examine this air diffuser to see if it is distorted or broken.

Not all circular wicks are of the central draught type. Kosmos burners—a name you will see on many small hand lamps and reading lamps—have flat wicks that come out circular in the burner. No diffuser is needed for this type of burner, as the draught is taken from the sides as in the ordinary flat-wick type.

The oil used in Argand lamps—colza oil or rape-seed oil—was obtained from the crushed seeds of brassica or kale, and gave a clear flame without much smoke or smell. It was also easy to store as it did not evaporate or deteriorate quickly. But it was sticky and heavy, and unless the lamps were cleaned regularly the burners tended to gum up. So when eventually paraffin or kerosene lamps were available side by side in the shops in the late nineteenth century, the paraffin lamp won the day due to its simplicity, reliability and the cheapness of its fuel.

36

Right: Early 19th century student's lamp. Adjustable. The colza oil was fed to the lamp from the reservoir by gravity. *Collection: F. Penny*

Left: Simple brass oil lamp with a central draught burner. The air is drawn through the pierced slits just below the reservoir. *Collection: Author*

Left: Student's oil lamp in copper and brass, with an unusual reflector.

Right: Three-feet high heater lamp with a magnificent pink cranberry glass shade that provides a really cosy glow. *Collection: F. Penny*

Metal based oil lamp with fine relief decoration.

Blue and white jasper ware lamp base, with etched glass shade. *Collection: F. Penny*

Left: One of the cheaper type of oil lamps. The reservoir is of painted metal with a printed design.

Right: A fine table lamp with ornate brass base. *Collection: F. Penny*

A pair of simple brass table lamps with attractive shades.
Photo: Libra Antiques

Left: Elaborately sculpted copper and brass oil lamp with frosted glass shade.

Right: Attractive European porcelain cherub holding oil lamp above his head. Cut glass reservoir. *Collection: F. Penny*

A GLOW FROM THE GUSHERS

~~~~~~

It was a combination of Scottish inventive genius and American enterprise that really launched the era of the kerosene or paraffin lamp, at the start of Queen Victoria's reign. The Scotsman was James Young, who developed a process of refining shale oil to produce paraffin in 1847, and used his new fuel to illuminate Riddings coal mine at Alfreton in Derbyshire. He patented his process in 1850, and founded a company called Young's Paraffin Oil Company to produce the distilled mineral oil from shale in the Scottish Lowlands. His company was eventually taken over by the British Petroleum Company, one of today's petrol giants. So Young was in fact the founder of the modern oil industry (although he had not truly been the first man to discover paraffin—that honour goes to Reichenbach and Dr Christison in 1830).

The potential of the new fuel was not universally recognised, except in Germany, and the earliest paraffin lamps came from there. At first the main supplies of the new mineral oil came from Burma and Romania, but it was quite expensive—which is probably why the fuel did not catch on quickly, in spite of its superiority over all other lamp oils. In the end it was the Americans who made cheap and abundant supplies of the fuel for the world's lamps possible. In 1859 New York imported 10,000 gallons of expensive Burmese oil and it was natural that prospectors should search for their own oil in a land so rich in natural resources.

So that same year, twelve years after Young's first experiments in Derbyshire, a lawyer called George H. Bissell sent out 'Colonel' Edwin L. Drake, an adventurous fellow willing to try his hand at anything, to test for oil on a large scale in Pennsylvania, where it was known that oil existed in natural wells. 'Colonel' Drake began his search in May 1858, and success came in August the following year when a well he had drilled, 69 feet deep, filled with oil. In the first

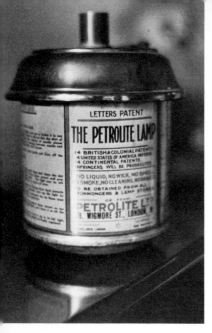

Right: A type of standard lamp with table platform that was popular in Edwardian times. The unusual feature of this lamp is that the fuel used was petrol.

Above: The special fuel container for the petrol lamp right. Although petrol was extensively used for lamps in America, there were few examples in Europe, where it was considered to be dangerous. *Collection: F. Penny*

day he pumped 25 barrels. The news spread rapidly and prospectors rushed to the area, called Oil Creek, to buy or lease land. By the end of 1860 there were 70 wells in the area and more than half a million barrels had been produced. But not all the men who sought fortunes in Oil Creek struck it rich: it wasn't long before oil prospecting was proved a dangerous occupation and 19 men were killed in an explosion after a huge new gusher was struck early in 1861.

In 1862 a young man called John D. Rockefeller began to lay the foundations of a huge fortune. He formed a company to refine the petroleum being pumped by the hundreds of different companies in the Oil Creek area. By 1870 he was such a dominant figure in the oil industry that he founded the Standard Oil Company, arranging with the railways for special cheap freight charges. It was not long before Rockefeller controlled 90 percent of the refineries, and in 1879 the United States, which 20 years earlier had been importing Burmese oil, was exporting 350 million gallons. These seemingly inexhaustible supplies from the American oilfields were shipped all round the world to go into lamps which gave light to humble cottage and royal palace alike. There was no serious challenge to American dominance of the industry until the twentieth century.

At this period of the nineteenth century, more than 80 patents every year were being taken out for new devices to improve oil lamps. And without doubt, one of the most important of these devices was the duplex burner, invented by Joseph Hicks, an Englishman. This burner had two flat wicks side by side, and an extinguisher device. The duplex burner was the most successful ever made, and is still produced today with the basic design unchanged.

Chimney shapes on the other hand varied with every type of burner, and there was a great deal of experiment to find the shape that suited each individual lamp best—the duplex burner, for example, was fitted with a chimney with an oval bulge, and the two wicks were fitted parallel with the bulge. Correctly shaped glass chimneys were found to be essential to obtain the best performance from a lamp.

But these chimneys were extremely fragile and there were places and occasions for which they were not really practicable. It was obviously pointless, for instance, to ship out chimneys for every

A splendid tall table lamp in blue and white continental faience.
Collection: F. Penny

45

Left: European porcelain base, with figure of a cherub holding a torch, which forms the lamp reservoir.

Right: A Sèvres porcelain ormolu-mounted lamp with its contemporary shade. This six-foot high lamp sold for £2000 at Bonhams, London.

Left: Fine china vase lamp, on brass base.

Right: Corinthian pillar combined with clear glass reservoir and shade make this a very attractive lamp. *Collection: F. Penny*

Left: Small table lamp on brass pedestal, with cut glass reservoir and etched frosted glass shade. *Collection: F. Penny*

Right: Late Victorian pottery lamp with hand-painted flowers and foliage and frosted glass shade. *Collection: Joan and Fred Crickard*

lamp to be used by British troops sent out to control the natives in remote corners of the Empire, for it was futile to expect that a consignment of glass chimneys would reach a border post of the North West frontier of India intact. So there were a variety of different inventions designed to make oil lamps work effectively without a chimney or a glass shade, by using a clockwork fan. The Hitchcock lamp, patented by Robert Hitchcock in New York in 1880, was one of the first and most successful. The Army and Navy Stores catalogue for 1907 describes it like this:

The Hitchcock Lamp is constructed on correct scientific principles, and burns without a chimney. A clockwork with a fan placed within the standard of the lamp drives a steady flow of air

Left: A pretty small bedroom oil lamp with cranberry glass reservoir on three clear glass feet. *Collection: Pam Penny*

Right: An unusual shaped China oil lamp on brass base, with white glass shade. *Collection: F. Penny*

Left: European porcelain oil lamp with ormolu handles and hand-painted scene.

Centre: European porcelain oil lamp with brass mounts, and exceptionally fine hand-painted shade.

Right: A fine china lamp with a splendid etched glass shade. *Collection: F. Penny*

upwards around the fount, keeping the oil in the fount cool; loose key to wind at side.

The purpose of the current of air, of course, was not so much to keep the oil cool as to provide a draught to stimulate the flame. Other types of chimneyless lamps were the Wanzer and the Brittanic. One advantage they had over lamps with a chimney was that they could be used for cooking as well as for lighting. They were rarely used in private homes, however, because of the risk of fire.

Many oil lamps made after 1885 had incandescent mantles similar to those used for gas lamps. The inventor of these mantles was Dr Carl Auer von Welsbach of Vienna, a pupil of Bunsen—whose name is known to every schoolboy. Welsbach's mantles were made of silk or cotton fabric impregnated with a mixture containing thorium and cerium, and if they were suspended in any flame—the fuel was irrelevant—they produced a very bright light. Many mantle burners had a duplex fitting, so that anyone with a duplex oil lamp could convert it by changing the burner. Incandescent mantles were only really successful with oil lamps when used with an oil vapour lamp like the one produced by Kitson in 1885, and many incandescent oil lamps had a special fuel pump which ensured that vaporised fuel was supplied steadily under pressure to the mantle. In some the burners are heated with methylated spirit flames before lighting.

Many pressure lamps are petrol burning, like the Coleman lamp which originated in Canada and was widely used throughout America, where petrol was cheap. Petrol was really regarded as a fairly useless substance in the nineteenth century, and it was never liked as a lighting fuel in Europe, where it was considered too dangerous. An advertisement for the Petrolite lamp in the 1907 Army and Navy Stores catalogue claims that it

burns petrol or motor spirit, is perfectly safe if instructions sent with each lamp are carried out. A lever controls the lighting arrangements; it gives a light of 50 candle power, and no wick is required.

The cost, complete with mantle, chimney and shade gallery was £1. 12s 6d (£1.62$\frac{1}{2}$). In the same catalogue, Read's patent Incandescent Petroleum Oil Burner ('Can be used with any duplex lamp') was priced 7s 9d (38p).

Left: Swans float gracefully around the etched glass shade of this lamp.

Centre: Hand-painted European porcelain vase shaped oil lamp with ormolu base and lion's head handles.

Right: The best feature here is the splendid shape. *Collection: F. Penny*

A DIVERSITY OF DECORATION

A fanatical collector friend of mine spends a great deal of his spare time touring junk shops and antique markets with one eye always cocked for old china 'vases'. The other eye, so to speak, is at the same time on the look-out for discarded oil lamp fittings that are going cheap because no one can find the old lamp that they will fit. But Fred can find a use for them—and for those old 'vases'.

China collectors like to buy vases in pairs, just as they like to buy china figures in pairs. A single example is never as easy to sell as a matching pair, so finely decorated vases, especially from the late Victorian and Edwardian periods which are not yet fully appreciated, can often be bought quite cheaply. What most china collectors do not realise is that many of these single vases were not made as vases at all. They started out as the bases of quite expensive oil lamps intended for the drawing rooms and dining rooms of the 1880s, 1890s and early 1900s. But when the great majority of homes were electrified (and that was a long drawn-out process covering decades) the old-fashioned lamps were scorned as useless and obsolete and the oil reservoirs, burners, shades and chimneys were often discarded. But not the pretty china bases—many housewives found a place for them in the home, as vases for flowers from the garden.

Fred can recognise any vase that was originally the base of an oil lamp instantly, by the shape of the top, into which a reservoir to contain oil was originally fitted. And when he isn't out looking for bargains he is likely to be in his workshop fitting the bases together with his other bits and pieces to make complete oil lamps, looking very much, perhaps occasionally even exactly, the same as they did when they were first bought from the shops two or three generations ago.

If relegation to the windowsill to hold bunches of Michaelmas daisies or dahlias was the fate of many china lamps, many lamps

Top left: A good hand lamp in brass. Essential in large houses to light the way down unlit corridors. *Collection: Eve Lane*
Top right: To light you to bed. This small cranberry glass oil lamp has a clear glass handle. *Collection: Pam Penny*
Bottom left: A fine brass hand lamp, with attractive etched glass shade.
Bottom right: Attractive small hand lamp with painted decoration and etched glass shade. *Collection: F. Penny*

A magnificent rise-and-fall oil lamp with cast brass supports and a white glass shade. The compensating weight ensures that the lamp will remain at whatever height is required. The tear drop glass lustres are an unusual feature. Circa 1890.
Collection: Noreen Baldock

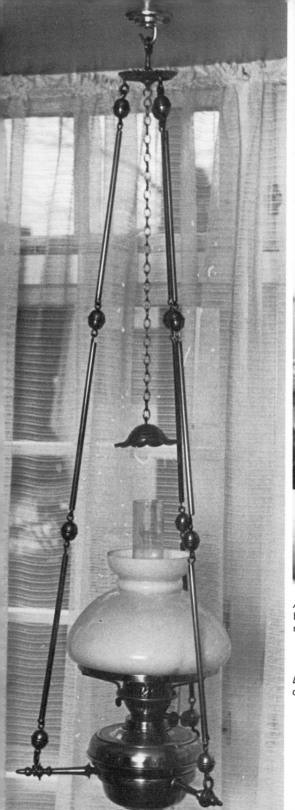

Above: Classical late 19th century oil lamp with brass Corinthian pillar and amethyst glass reservoir. *Collection: Gwen Hughes*

Left: An attractive hanging brass church lamp. 19th century. *Collection: Noreen Baldock*

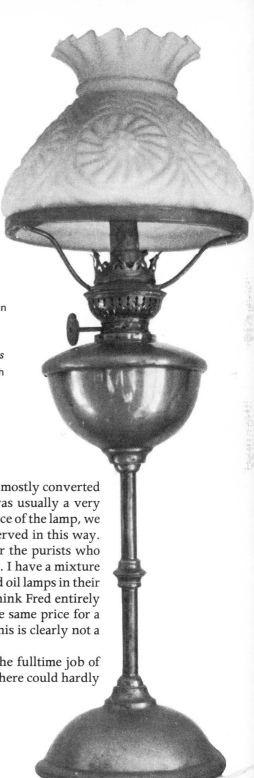

Left: 19th century German porcelain group put to splendid use as the base for an electric table lamp.
Collection: Gwen Hughes

Right: Small oil lamp with brass reservoir and base and copper pillar. The shade is an attractive peacock blue at the top, shading down to white. Converted for electricity.
Collection: Author

made of metal suffered a different fate—they were mostly converted to take electrical fittings. Since this conversion was usually a very simple matter and rarely altered the basic appearance of the lamp, we can only be grateful that so many have been preserved in this way. There are still plenty of unconverted oil lamps for the purists who might sniff at anything that is not entirely original. I have a mixture of lamps that have been converted to electricity and oil lamps in their original state in my own home, although I don't think Fred entirely approves. Antique shops seem to charge much the same price for a converted lamp as for one in its original form, so this is clearly not a point that worries most collectors.

At least the converted lamps are being put to the fulltime job of lighting homes that they were intended for—and there could hardly

Left: A sturdy brass harp lamp, with white glass shade. Converted for electricity. *Collection: Author*

Right: A fine hanging lamp. *Collection: Noreen Baldock*

Hanging lantern for a hall or passageway. The four glass panels, cut and engraved through a ruby casing, are encased by a copper frame. Access to the small oil lamp inside is simple—just pull the bottom ring and the lamp is lowered while the casing rises on the copper chains. *Collection: Author*

be a place even in today's expanding world for all the old oil lamps of the past unless some of them were put to practical use. It is amazing to think now how many oil lamps a single large household might have possessed in the nineteenth century. In the wealthier homes there might be as many as 40, and it must have been almost a fulltime job for one of the servants to keep the brassware brightly polished, the wicks trimmed or replaced when necessary, the reservoirs topped with oil, and the chimneys and globes washed and polished.

Let's consider the lamps even the ordinary home would need. In the drawing room and the dining room there would be either duplex lamps or 50-candlepower central draught lamps, probably made in china by one of the leading factories of the day if they were table

58

Old 19th century lamp bases in white Dresden china, awaiting restoration to their original purpose.

Adjustable wall lamp on a swing bracket. *Collection: F. Penny*

Left: Green-glazed china oil lamp with double horses' heads, and applied white relief decoration.

Right: Porcelain cherubs make a splendid base for this 19th century oil lamp. *Collection: F. Penny*

Fine oil lamp on a tall brass Corinthian pillar, supporting a cradle for the cut-glass bowl. Green shade. *Collection: F. Penny*

lamps, or of brass on tall pedestals if they were standard lamps. Some of the more ornate standard lamps would incorporate a small circular table at waist height. The pillars might be made of brass, wrought iron or wood and were usually partly telescopic for some height adjustment. In the kitchen there would probably be a hanging lamp of some sort and at least one fairly plain brass lamp with a one-inch flat wick or a Kosmos burner. Small flat-wick lamps with a carrying handle were the usual illumination for bedrooms and there might be bracket lamps on the walls of the bathroom and lavatory.

Naturally the lady of the house would want even such utilitarian necessities as lamps to look decorative, and to fit in with her furnishing scheme. A glance through the catalogues of Victorian and Edwardian stores will reveal a bewildering selection of lamps and shades; it was usual for the buyer first to choose her lamp, and then a shade to match her decor at home.

The cheapest sort of table lamp found in the stores of those days would have a fount of opal glass decorated with transfer-printed flowers and a cast iron stand. Next step up in the price range was the lamp with a shiny black china base and a brass pillar holding a reservoir in coloured fluted glass—red, amber, green or blue, perhaps. Or instead of the brass pillar there might be a coloured china or glass pillar supporting a reservoir of clear glass. Some especially splendid lamps had cut-glass founts, mounted on the popular and impressive Corinthian pillars in brass, copper or silver plate.

Apart from these lamps, there were, of course, reading lamps for the library and study, and lamps for playing billiards by—one type consisted of a suspended ceiling fitting with arms for four independent oil lamps with cut glass reservoirs and green shades to throw the light downwards on the table and keep it out of the eyes of the players.

Hanging lamps were made in a wide variety of shapes. The cheapest and most commonly used was the simple harp lamp with a

Left: Tall oil lamp on a slender brass pillar, with milk glass reservoir and shade.

Right: Attractive matched pair of table lamps with cut glass bowls and original shades. *Collection: F. Penny*

wire frame and a japanned metal fount with a tin reflector, which was designed for use in church halls, schools, libraries and other assembly rooms where numbers of people might gather. Slightly more expensive harp lamps had a wrought iron frame, a larger japanned metal reflector and a glass fount. For the really high-class

Left: Fine cameo glass oil lamp, probably by Webb. Bright blue glass overlaid in white. The oil is carved with birds on a flowering branch, with a butterfly nearby. The shade is decorated with butterflies and insects above flowering branches.

Right: Rare cameo glass oil lamp by Webb, finely carved in white with a branch of cherry blossom and a butterfly on the lamp, which is supported on three frosted glass legs. *Photo: Phillips*

Far left: An ornate table oil lamp in silver plate, with a cherub supporting the etched glass oil reservoir. Tear-drop glass lustres. *Collection: Noreen Baldock*

Left: Colourful oil lamp with a blue glass and gilt metal support, a cut-glass reservoir and attractive cranberry pink shade. *Collection: Author*

Right: Pair of Doulton oil lamps by Lucy Barlow, decorated in pate sur pate with small birds in the branches of a tree. The handles, burner and three-hoofed foot are in gilt metal. Cut-glass chimneys and shades, 1883. *Photo: Sotheby's, London*

Doulton lamp by Mark Marshall. The stoneware vase section is supported by an elaborate ormolu base. *Collection: Shirley Vallance*

A really exceptional lamp. The female figure and reservoir are in Worcester porcelain. Circa 1900. *Collection: F. Penny*

Right: Magnificent mermaid lamp in Doulton faience. The mermaid, with pearls in her hair rises from sea-green waves and is entwined around branches of pink coral which support a beige and coral pink reservoir. Height 34 inches. *Collection: Author*

places the frame would be in brass with a brass fount and an opal glass or green glass shade.

Another more splendid type of hanging lamp was the suspension lamp. Instead of a rigid metal harp frame there was an arrangement of chains and pulleys so that the lamp could easily be lowered for filling and cleaning

The other main type of hanging lamp was for the hall or vestibule. It was suspended on chains and sometimes could also be lowered on pulleys. These hall lamps were often of the lantern type, consisting of a small oil lamp placed inside a surround of coloured or etched glass panels.

Swing bracket lamps were also used in halls and on landings, and

Left: Edwardian white pottery owl lamp, converted for electricity. Owl lamps were made in very large numbers, but are not easy to find now. *Collection: Joan and Fred Crickard*

Right: A hand-carved wooden bear supports this glass oil lamp. *Collection: F. Penny*

Left: Splendidly colourful kingfisher lamp base in china and applied beads.

Right: Another member of the oil lamp menagerie. This time a beady-eyed bat.
Collection: F. Penny

in railway carriages and caravans. The brackets were either of brass or iron and were available for all sizes and styles of burners. Some small bracket lamps were made to be screwed on to pianos. Another type of piano lamp was designed to fit into the candle sconces attached to the piano.

For the really well-to-do all the leading glass and china manufacturers competed to make ornamental lamps for the luxury end of the market. As we have already seen, many of the china lamps have since been broken up, so the oil lamps that seem to bring the highest prices in the sale rooms today are those made of art glass by craftsmen such as Galle and Webb, who specialised in beautiful cameo glass, which was sometimes used both for the bowls and shades of oil lamps. The most famous example of cameo glass is the reproduction of the Portland vase made in England by John Northwood of Wordsley. Such pieces were made by 'casing' an opal glass on to a body of either clear or coloured glass, then carving away the outer layer so that the design stood out in relief. Not quite so intricate, and therefore not so expensive, was the cased glass made in Bohemia, and also at Stourbridge in England. Here again a layer of coloured glass was 'cased' over clear glass. Then a design was cut into the outer layer so that the clear layer underneath showed through and provided the pattern: in this case the effect was intaglio rather than relief like the cameo carving. This kind of decorated Bohemian glass was frequently used for the glass panels in hall lanterns.

Of the china lamps there were many splendid ones made by the old-established firms such as Minton and Wedgwood, and by the art potteries. Perhaps the most outstanding example of the latter was the revitalised Doulton firm, whose master craftsmen and women, such as Mark Marshall and Hannah Barlow, brought it such renown that new Doulton china is probably the most widely collected of all pottery of the late nineteenth and early twentieth centuries.

Tiny novelty oil lamps, shaped as a fireplace, rocking chair and gramophone. Circa 1910. *Collection F. Penny*

Not all china lamps were of simple vase shapes: there was a great
vogue for lamps in animal and bird shapes—elephants, bears, bats,
and almost certainly the most popular of all, owls. Owl lamps were
made in huge numbers and in many different sizes. My own
favourite figurative lamp is one made in Doulton faience at Burslem,

70

Satsuma lamp with
extravagant ormolu
base and fine etched
glass shade.
Collection: F. Penny

representing a mermaid rising from the waves, with pearl beads in her hair, supporting the reservoir of the oil lamp on branches of pink coral.

When collectors come across old oil lamps there are often parts missing, and to many people replacing these parts might seem an impossible task. So it is heartening to know that there is now a comprehensive spare parts service for old oil lamps run by Christopher Wray at his Lamp Workshop in Kings Road, London. Many of the parts are made in Mr Wray's own workshop, with tools and equipment he has rescued from the premises of former manufacturers in Birmingham. If you think you may not have the correct chimney for your lamp you can choose from 150 different types. There are also shades in several different shapes and colours, not just the green or white that were available a few years ago. But if you do have an old oil lamp with its original shade, do take care of it. A genuine old shade considerably increases the value of any lamp. Old shades are always of thinner glass than the modern repro-ductions, and were made in a great number of different shapes and decorative designs that are no longer available. Having an old chimney is not of such importance: this is in any case likely to have been replaced several times in the life of a lamp, being liable at some stage to crack through contact with the flame.

Left: European porcelain cherub clutching cut glass oil lamp reservoir, with narrow glass funnel.

Right: Another attractive cherub oil lamp. *Collection: F. Penny*

China elephant oil
lamp with an etched
glass shade.
Collection: F. Penny

TO GUIDE THE TRAVELLER

The lantern has always been the lamp for out-of-doors, the guiding light of the traveller. It seems to have been devised by the Romans, who placed an oil lamp inside a copper or bronze frame with windows made either of translucent horn or of bladder, to prevent the flame from being blown out by the wind. Mugging was as rife in Rome in those days as it is in modern cities today and few people dared venture out after dark. So when rich citizens found it absolutely necessary to move about the streets at night, they were always accompanied by guards, some of them bearing lanterns before them. It is known for instance that Mark Antony had his own personal lantern-bearer. When the distinguished Roman came under suspicion of plotting with Caesar's enemies, his unfortunate servant was tortured in an attempt to make him reveal whom his master had visited under cloak of darkness.

Beautiful copper and bronze lanterns were discovered when Pompeii and Herculaneum were first excavated in the eighteenth century. One of the finest of these was cylindrical and made of sheet copper, except for the two main supports by which it was suspended. These were cast iron. The lantern had a removable hemispherical top, punctuated with air holes, and the base consisted of a flat, circular copper plate supported by three balls and turned up all round the rim. The top and base were connected by the cast rectangular supports and also by interior uprights, framing the horn windows. A small oil lamp was placed in the centre of the lantern.

The Romans used both hand and hanging lanterns. Later European lanterns, like the Roman ones, had either horn or bladder windows, but the lighting agent was more often a candle than an oil lamp. Thin sheets of horn remained popular for lantern windows right through the Middle Ages and into the middle of the nineteenth century, because horn was less liable to break than glass—it is

Left: Railway reading lamp, 19th century. Put a penny in the slot and push the button . . . *Photo: Crown copyright, Science Museum, London*

Right: Multi-purpose railway lamp, standard issue for London and North Eastern Railway stations in England and Scotland. This one has a brass plate inscribed with the name of the station: Hatfield.

significant that the old English word for lantern was *lant-horn.* Mica or oiled paper was also sometimes used in Europe for the window sections, while in China, Persia and Japan lanterns were made of silk or paper. Many of these were collapsible, with a metal top and base, and were intended for the traveller to hang in his tent at night.

The most primitive lanterns are the clay lanterns of Africa, and the all-metal lanterns with perforated sides which continued to be used in Europe for hundreds of years. Most of the illuminating power was obscured by the metal sides but these lanterns did have the merit of durability, and they were made in considerable numbers, in either

76

sheet iron or bronze, throughout Europe. These were less common in Britain than in other European countries, with the exception of the nightguard type containing a rush light, which was often placed in British bedrooms in the eighteenth and nineteenth centuries. Charles Dickens clearly did not have a high regard for them, and one wonders whether they were worth having at all, after reading Pip's description of a night away from home in *Great Expectations*:

As I had asked for a nightlight, the chamberlain brought me in, before he left me, the good old constitutional rushlight of those virtuous days—an object like the ghost of a walking cane, which instantly broke its back if it were touched, which nothing could ever be lighted at, and which was placed in solitary confinement at the bottom of a high tin tower, perforated with round holes that made a staringly wide-awake pattern on the walls. When I had got

Large brass ship's lamp with red glass, circa 1910, and sister lamp with clear glass.

Acetylene lamp, probably for a motor cycle. *Collection: F. Penny*

into bed, and lay there footsore, weary, and wretched, I found that I could no more close my own eyes than I could close the eyes of this foolish Argus. And thus, in the gloom and death of the night, we stared at one another.

What a doleful night! How anxious, how dismal! How long!

And how extraordinary that this type of lighting remained in such widespread use for so long!

More attractive perforated and openwork lamps, even if the illumination they gave was also minimal, were made in the near and Middle Eastern countries, usually of brass or bronze and cylindrical in form. Some Persian examples however were shaped like a complete sphere with a candle socket in the base and an opening at the top. A curious variation of this round Persian lantern is the rolling lantern. If it is knocked or pushed it will just roll over a little way, and then stop, the perforated holes in the metalwork acting as a brake as well as a base. Meanwhile the central burner oil lamp inside remains upright in the centre of a series of metal rings forming a gimbal.

When glass first started to be used for lantern windows in Europe, some lanterns had glass front windows only and others had glass on

all sides. The value of bullseye glass as a magnifying lens was appreciated from the beginning of the eighteenth century, and many bullseye lanterns were made.

But however serviceable a simple lantern carried in the hand might be for the traveller on foot, it was not very satisfactory for people who wanted to move more swiftly by night, and the sensible traveller carried his own collapsible lamp to set up in his room at the inn or to light up the interior of his carriage. This sort of lamp has been known since the sixteenth century. In one form a screw cap fits

King of the Road acetylene lamp by Lucas, for car or motorcycle. *Collection: F. Penny*

79

over the wick to prevent the oil spilling, and the lantern glass slides over the reservoir body when the lamp is not in use. There is often a recess to contain tweezers for adjusting and trimming the wick. Another type, which came into use among rail travellers in the nineteenth century, is the spring-loaded candle-holder which has sharp prongs for fitting to the seat back, and which can be folded flat against the candle-holder when not in use.

Such lamps would have been very useful for anyone travelling by horse bus. Like railway carriages these were at first completely unlit, and even after 1853 when lighting for passengers became a requirement before a licence to run a horse bus could be granted, it was usually a simple small colza oil lamp hung inside the door. When the door was opened the interior of the horse bus was in almost total darkness. These lamps were supplied to London horse bus companies by James Willing for a fee of fourpence a day, which the conductor was obliged to pay out of his takings. Around 1890 there were several experiments in lighting the horse buses by electric light, and the newspapers promised travellers the replacement of 'dim and smoky oil lamps' by 'bright and cleanly electric light', so that 'Londoners can now read the evening papers with comfort on the journey to their homes.' But the London Omnibus Carriage Co. Ltd decided that the electric lighting was too expensive, and although acetylene and paraffin lamps were used in horse buses in the early years of this century, they were still dim and gloomy.

Railway travellers did fare a little better, and most of the railway companies provided light for the traveller—although sometimes he had to pay for it. Some companies fitted electric coin-in-the-slot reading lamps in their carriages. The falling penny switched on the lamp and also activated a timing device. There was a refund chute and a button for putting out the light. You could switch it on again by pressing a different button to use up the rest of your pennyworth.

The first lighting in trains was, of course, by oil lamps, and Queen Victoria happily travelled backwards and forwards to Balmoral in

Small oil lamp for early
20th century bicycle.
Collection: F. Penny

Railwayman's signal lamp. Just a little twist and the light changes from red to green.
Collection: F. Penny

compartments lit in this way: so happily in fact that when the North Western Company installed gas lighting in the royal carriages she was not amused. She sent her trusty servant John Brown to tell the company that she required the immediate removal of the gas lights and the return of the old oil lamps and candles. Change for change's sake did not suit the old Queen, and when the Great Western Railway built a completely new royal train for the Diamond Jubilee in 1897, complete with all mod cons and electric lighting, the Queen insisted that there should be no interference at all with the personal carriage in which she normally travelled. So while she agreed to the new train being built, she herself travelled in a carriage 23 years older than the rest, still lit by a huge cloche-shaped oil lamp in the centre of the domed ceiling.

The railways, of course, needed many different kinds of lights and it would be easy for a collector to specialise in railway lamps alone. Lamps were made for many specific purposes—for the engines, the rolling stock, signals, crossings, platforms and so on. Each separate railway company would have its own designs and the railway enthusiast will look for different lamps bearing the name or initials of the Great Western Railway, the London Midland and Scottish, the London and North Eastern and all the others. A good place to start a collection of railway lamps is British Rail's Collectors' Corner near Euston Station in London, where a selection of obsolete railway equipment and ephemera is available for sale.

Collectors interested in sailing and the sea will want to have a few ship lamps in their homes, and the old oil lamps in copper or brass are often very impressive. You can look for the triangular lights marked Port and Starboard. Then there are binnacle lamps, bulkhead lanterns in a variety of shapes and sizes, berth lanterns, cargo lanterns, engine room lanterns and signalling lamps. Many lamps carry the name of the vessel on which they were used.

Another field in which a collector could specialise is that of coach, bicycle and automobile lamps. The earliest coach lamps were simple lanterns containing candles or small oil lamps. In the eighteenth and nineteenth centuries, there were considerable variations in shape, ranging from simple rectangular lamps in black japanned metal for horse carts, to splendid brass lamps with cut glass windows for the carriages of the rich. There were also footboard lanterns—and in the catalogue of the Army and Navy Stores for 1907 there are even 'patent stirrup lamps' for horsemen. These cost 19 shillings and, according to the catalogue, were 'very useful for horsemen at night; they give a powerful light, are simple in construction, and can be attached instantly to any ordinary stirrups, thus forming a security and protection to all horsemen'.

The first cycling lamps were oil lamps or candle lamps, but the advent of acetylene improved the lighting power tremendously. Acetylene is produced by adding water to calcium carbide and the Army and Navy Stores catalogue warned: 'Carbide being classified as a dangerous article cannot be sent by Post or Passenger Train but can be supplied to Members personally in 1lb tins.' The fuel was discovered by Moissan in 1892 when he was conducting experiments to manufacture artificial diamonds. He did not make any diamonds, but the new carbide fuel provided lighting for bicycles, and later for automobiles, for 30 years.

Below and overleaf:
Early automobile acetylene lamps, still in use on vintage vehicles.
Photos: Christies, London

CONVERTING THE CANDLE

There was a strange fad in the eighteenth century among people who liked gimmicks for the 'clock lamp', by which it was possible to tell the time, more or less accurately. The timing device was a tall metal table lamp with a glass reservoir marked with lines representing the hours. As the lamp burned, the level of the oil fell and the lamp's owner could see how much time had elapsed. The Saxon King Alfred had used more or less the same idea some centuries earlier, but with better reason: reliable mechanical clocks were unknown in his time. King Alfred's way of telling the time was to have candles made of an established weight and length and to have each of them marked with 12 divisions. When the candles burned each division represented 20 minutes, and it required six of his candles to complete one day. Charles V of France is said to have done things on a bigger scale—he always had a time candle in his chapel that would last the full 24 hours.

The history of the candle goes back to Roman times, and by the Middle Ages the use of candles was widespread, chiefly because they were much cheaper to run than oil lamps and gave roughly the same illumination. Even after the introduction of the Argand lamp in the eighteenth century the candle was not ousted—ordinary people could not afford the expensive colza oil which the Argand lamp devoured so voraciously. The wax candle was itself too expensive for the poorer people, who preferred to use tallow candles, made in the home by melting animal fats. The tallow candle would often give as good a light as a wax candle for about ten minutes, but then it would grow dimmer and dimmer, and it also gave off an offensive smell. Nevertheless it was still in use in the second half of the nineteenth century.

Even the wax candles of those days, made of beeswax, did not give as bright a light as the modern candle. There was some

improvement in the eighteenth century when a substance called *spermaceti*, from the sperm whale, was used in the manufacture of candles. The term one candle-power, which came to be the basic measure of light, was based on the illumination given by a single spermaceti candle. Twentieth-century candles, containing paraffin wax, are brighter.

There have been a number of devices described as lamps in which in fact a candle was the source of light. The description can be justified because in most of them the illumination was intensified by a reflector or some other means. The true lacemakers' lamp, for example, consisted of a small table with an adjustable candlestick for a tallow candle in the centre. The candlestick was surrounded by four spherical glass bowls which were kept filled with water. The light from the candle, diffused and magnified through the waterfilled bowls, gave a steady, even and fairly bright light for a number of lacemakers around the table to work by. This device was also used by jewellers, engravers and others who wanted to perform delicate work by night. Distilled spirit was added to the water to keep it clear.

In the nineteenth century a large number of different candle lamps were manufactured, many of them of the night light type. These were a great improvement on the earlier cheerless perforated metal lanterns for rush lights described by Dickens in *Great Expectations*. The night light was usually placed on a glass dish set on a pedestal, with a glass cover over it. Some of these night light covers made in Germany and Switzerland carried etched or painted domestic scenes or flowers. Covers made in Britain were often of satin glass, pink cranberry glass, or attractively striped and swirled. One of the main manufacturers from about 1860 onwards was Samuel Clarke of London, who introduced a special slow-burning safety candle for these night lights. Clarke used a fairy with a wand as his trade mark, along with the words 'Clarke's Patented Cricklite'. Some of his night lights have the words 'Fairy Light' or 'Pyramid' on them. There were also the very appealing little pottery cottages made in Staffordshire and at Rockingham, each with an open front and a chimney, which are today so sought after by china collectors.

One very attractive candle lamp made from about 1770 was really an improved form of the bedroom candlestick. It had a high glass

Far left: A splendid pair of ormolu candelabra converted for electricity.

Left: A Loetz iridescent glass candle lamp. The 'mob cap' shade is supported on a simulated candle, set in a twisted and fluted base. The glass is decorated with dappled pale green, gold and pink iridescence. The pontil is engraved Loetz, Austria. Circa 1900. *Photo: Sotheby's, London*

Right: Unusual oil lamp with glass stem and a beaded shade. Circa 1910. *Collection: F. Penny*

funnel, which slotted into the body and gave a steady, even flame even in draughty passages. The metal body was pierced below the glass funnel to create a draught of air for the flame. Like the conventional chamber candlestick, this candle lamp had a snuffer which had a specially long handle so that it could reach down inside the glass. The lamp bases might be made of silver, Sheffield plate, electroplate or brass, and some particularly attractive examples had glass globes instead of the usual sleeve-like funnels.

One form of student's lamp was a metal candle lamp with a hooded reflector, so that the light was concentrated on the books being read. The candle was held in a metal tube in which there was a spring that kept the candle in position as the wax melted away. These remained in use until Edwardian times, when the simplest variety, nickel-plated all over, could be bought for eight shillings. Another aid to students and others who wanted to read by night without wasting money on the expensive midnight oil, was a candleshield, patented in 1817. This was a fan-like shield which opened into a complete circle and was placed in such a position that the candlelight fell on the pages of the book but did not shine in the student's eyes, thereby reducing eye strain.

There were other candle lamps without the hooded reflector, such as Green's Patent Arctic Lamps for Candles, for which frilly shades could be purchased. A London store catalogue describes it like this:

The 'Arctic' Lamp is constructed on the same principle as a carriage or reading lamp, in which the candle, enclosed in a metal tube, is forced up as it burns by means of a spiral spring inside. It fits in any ordinary candlestick and is made to exactly resemble a wax candle when in use. Ordinary candle shades can be used with perfect safety. The candles always remain the same height, yet are burned to the end without the slightest waste.

The catalogue shows illustrations of a fashionable Edwardian lady reading in bed by means of the Arctic lamp fitted in a brass bracket attached to the bed, and a man shaving with a cut-throat razor, his candle lamp attached to the looking glass with a similar bracket. The Arctic Lamp was also available with a piano fitting. The fancy fabric shades for this type of candle lamp had a wire frame which fitted over the metal tube containing the candle.

A dual purpose form of lighting for the desk came in the forms of

An attractive Tiffany Studios candle lamp. The fluted bell-form shade is in opaque glass with an overall pale gold lustre. *Photo: Sotheby's, London*

89

the waxjack and the *bougie* box. Both held a coil of wax taper. The waxjack has a metal frame with a horizontal bar which has a coiled length of taper around it. The end of this taper projects through a small nozzle at the top or is held by a spring clip. In the bougie box the coil is contained in a small drum-shaped box about three inches high and is pulled through a hole in the centre of the lid. The box, usually made of brass, silver or silver plate, may be plain or decorated by piercing and chasing. There is a handle and, as with the waxjacks, a matching extinguisher. These were also intended for melting sealing wax and perhaps lighting pipes and cigars.

Left: Tiffany Studios candle lamp with a tapered six-sided iridescent gold glass shade on a bronze tripod stem. Circa 1910. *Photo: Sotheby's, London*

Right: Candle lamps for sale: A page from an Edwardian Army and Navy Stores catalogue.

The "Queen."

READING LAMPS FOR OIL AND CANDLE.

Candle Reading Lamp.
Telescopic Corrugated Hood.

Hooded Lamp for Petroleum Oil.

Hooded Piano Lamp.

Candle Reading Lamp.

The "Queen" Reading Lamp, no. 1,
brass, for mineral oil, with white
shade 11/3
No. 2, nickel-plated, for mineral oil,
with white shade 13/6
Extra shades for do., white 0/7;
green 1/5 ; pink 1/8
Chimneys, best quality .... doz 4/8
Wicks .... pkt 0/3
No. 3, nickel-plated, for colza oil,
with white shade 13/6
Extra shades for do., white, 0/7; green,
1/4 ; pink 2/0
Chimneys, best quality .... doz 4/0
Wicks .... pkt 0/3
No. 5, "Queen's," with two burners,
nickel plated, for mineral oil, with
white shades 21/3
Extra shades for do., each, white 0/7 ;
green, 1/5 ; pink 1/8
Chimneys, best quality .... doz 4/8
Wicks .... pkt 0/3
No. 7, "Queen's" two burners, nickel
plated, for colza, two white shades 21/3
Extra shades for do., white, 0/7;
green, 1/4 ; pink 2/0
Chimneys, best quality .... doz 4/0
Wicks .... pkt 0/3

Nickel-plated all over 13/0
Electro-plated all over 23/6
Candles for above, box of 6 1/3½

Special Reading Lamp.

With Duplex Burner.

No. 2705.
10 line N. P. Lamp
with hood and chim-
ney complete 11/6

Railway Reading Lamps.

Nickel - plated,
square 5/8
Candles for do., box 0/8½
Railway Reading
Lamp, nickel-
plated, round 3/6
Leather Case for
square lamp 4/8
Leather Case for
round lamp 4/6

Nickel-plated 6/9

Wood case
for above,
with parti-
tions for
chimneys,
&c. 6/0

This case is with
glass divisions and
without, it is there-
fore necessary to
pack the goods for
travelling.

Nickel-plated
candlestick
with electro-
plated reflector 14/0

Short short 6
candles for do.,
2 lb. box 1/6

PATENT IMPROVED CHAMPION CANDLE SHADE HOLDER

Patent Self-descending Candle Shade Support, made for candles 4, 6, or 8, as shown
.... 0/9½ Nickel plated, 0/11
In ordering please state size.

Single stand, nickel-
plated, with 1 N.P.
Duplex burner, 1
cut glass container,
1 green shade and
chimney, as shown 38/9
Do., do., polished
brass stand and
burner 34/3
Extra Green Shades 2/9
Nickel-plated, with 2
arms, 2 N. P.
Duplex burners,
2 cut glass con-
tainers, 2 green
shades, and 2
Chimneys 53/4

Double Tube Candlestick, for Reading, &c. Corrugated Hood.

Takes short short 6
candles.
Electro-plated on
German silver 60/9
Do., E. P. hood,
N. P. stand 51/3
Single Wick Can-
dles, 2 lb. box 1/6
Double do. .... pkt 4/0

Candle Reading Lamp. (Telescopic.)

Nickel-plated all
over 8/3
E. P. all over 19/0
Candles for above,
box of 6 .... 1/3½

Corrugated Hood Candle Reading Lamp.

Electro - plated all
over 25/3
Nickel-plated stand,
with E. P. Hood .. 20/3
Silver do., to order
only £8 15 0
2 lb. box short short
6 candles for do. .. 1/6

In ordering chimneys and wicks for reading lamps it is necessary to state if for duplex, mineral, or colza oil.

SLOW GOING BY GASLIGHT

The ancient Chinese—weren't they always ahead of every other nation?—were the first people to experiment with lighting by gas. They are believed to have collected natural gas from 'fire wells' and to have stored it in animal bladders. When they wanted light they pricked holes in these containers and lit the jets of gas that issued from the the holes.

Thousands of years later, towards the end of the seventeenth century, similar fire wells were a cause of fear and wonder for the people who lived in certain parts of south Lancashire, and Thomas Shirley reported to the Royal Society in London that he had seen 'a well and earth taking fire at a candle' near Wigan. The simple local people believed that it was the water itself that was so frighteningly inflammable, but Shirley established that it was the bubbles of gas coming up through the water that caught fire. After drawing the water away from the well he was able apparently to set the earth alight. Later investigators demonstrated that the gas came from coal beds underground and succeeded in distilling gas from the coal. One of these scientists was a Dean Clayton of Kildare, who collected his gas in exactly the same way as the ancient Chinese, in animal bladders, and found that the light given from pin pricks in the bladders was superior to that of any lamps then in existence. Although he made these experiments in 1688, he did not follow them up and did not even publish his findings until more than 40 years later. A seventeenth-century French doctor, Jean Tardin, also intrigued by fire wells near Grenoble, traced the gas to local coal beds and succeeded in producing artificial gas by heating crushed coal in a closed vessel. Another Frenchman, called Jars, tried to pipe gas from a coalmine near Lyons in 1764, but his scheme ended in

A very attractive gas table lamp from about 1880. The milk glass shade is painted with birds and flowers. *Photo: Crown copyright, Science Museum, London*

disaster when the gas exploded.

The accolade for being the first man successfully to use gas for domestic lighting must go to a Mr Spedding, who managed Lord Lonsdale's colliery near Whitehaven on the Cumberland coast. Spedding lit his own offices by gas and offered to supply the streets of the town with similar lighting. The local magistrates refused to let him proceed with his scheme, thereby denying their town a very special place in history. That was nearly half a century before the first introduction of street lighting anywhere in the world—in London in 1807.

In the end it was that brilliant engineer Richard Murdoch who really established gas as a viable source of public and domestic lighting. In 1792 he distilled gas from coal in iron retorts at Redruth in Cornwall, and burned the gas at the end of an open tube. Then he had the inspired idea of closing the end of the tube and piercing holes in it to make an effective but primitive burner. Where did the inspiration come from? There is a romantic story, which could possibly be true, that one day he wanted to close the end of the open gas tube and the nearest thing to hand was one of his wife's thimbles. The well-used thimble had some holes in it and tiny jets of flame were produced through these.

Like Spedding, Murdoch lit his offices and home with gas. A few years later he used gas to light the Boulton and Watts foundry in Birmingham, and in 1802 he produced the forerunner of the modern neon advertising sign that brightens the world's cities today by using tiny gas jets to spell out the words 'Peace In Europe', celebrating the signing of the Peace of Amiens. His second successful commercial lighting venture was when he installed 900 lights at a cotton mill in Salford, Lancashire, and from then onwards the revolutionary new lighting was eagerly adopted by all the leading industrialists as soon as they had access to a supply of gas that could be piped to them.

Meanwhile an enterprising German called F. A. Winsor was turning the potential of gas lighting to his own advantage. In 1803 he had the Lyceum Theatre, London, lit by gas and organised lectures there to publicise the new lighting and his own plans to develop it.

Suspended ornamental gas lamp with inverted burner. *Photo: Crown copyright, Science Museum, London*

Quite untruthfully he claimed to be the inventor of gas lighting and invited his audiences to invest in his scheme for installing it in the streets of London. Winsor's chief aim was to make himself rich and he had prospectuses for 'The National Light and Heat Company' distributed, promising fantastic profits for anyone who would invest in it: £570 a year on a down payment of £5 for each of 20,000 £50 shares. His coal gas, he claimed without a blush, was 'more congenial to the lungs than oxygen'! But however dubious the German adventurer's intentions he did give great impetus to the establishment of gas lighting. He exhibited lights and a gas-lit transparency on the outside walls of his house in Pall Mall on King George IV's birthday, 4 June 1807, each lamp consisting of three gas jets in a glass globe. Two months later the Golden Lane Brewery installed 11 gas lamps each 20 yards apart in two streets next to the brewery. 'The single row of lamps fully illuminate both sides of the lane,' it was proudly announced. Winsor pressed on with his own venture and established The Chartered Company, the first such public company in the world, which became the Gas Light and Coke Company, and remained in business until it was absorbed by Britain's nationalised gas industry in 1948.

Its eventual success brought no joy for the first shareholders, however, who never received the fat profits they were originally promised. Gas lighting required a gas works to make and store the fuel and long expensive runs of piping that were uneconomic to provide unless a large number of customers were available in a fairly concentrated area. Capital expenditure was therefore heavy before reasonable returns were seen for the investment. But most of the world's leading cities followed London's example and installed gas

Attractive street lamp with copper 'roof'. Probably originally a gas lamp, converted to electricity.

96

lighting in the streets and in many homes—Dublin in 1818, Paris in 1819, Philadelphia in 1835 and Sydney, Australia, in 1841.

The first gas lights in the streets had to be turned on and lit separately, so the gas companies had to employ a team of lamplighters. These men carried round with them a ladder and a lantern from which they could light the gas burners. Later the ladder was dispensed with and each lamplighter carried a long wooden pole with a metal hook on the end for opening the hinged lamp window and turning on the gas tap. The flame was then lit by a simple oil lamp held aloft at the end of the lamplighter's pole.

Hundreds of different burners were experimented with, the earliest one in widespread use being the rat-tail, in which a single flame emerged from an orifice. But this was replaced in many lamps after 1808 by the cockspur burner, which gave a triple flame, and provided a light of one candle power for every cubic foot of gas burned per hour. Then came the cockscomb, with a larger number of holes, followed in 1816 by the batswing, which had a narrow slit in place of holes, and as its name suggests produced a flame shaped roughly like a bat's wing. Later there was the fishtail burner, in which two jets of gas united to create a single flame. Strangely, it was not until after Edison and Swan had produced their first successful domestic lighting that gas really became the standard lighting for most homes. By that time, of course, most towns had gas supplies and gas lighting was available for any of the townspeople who could afford it. When Dr von Welsbach produced his first incandescent mantle in 1884, providing greatly increased illumination, almost everyone wanted gas lighting. Welsbach's first incandescent gas mantle was placed upright in gas lights, as in oil lamps, but in 1905 the mantle was made shorter and inverted in all new gas lamps, so that the light was radiated downwards, where it was needed most.

The story of gas lighting, which began long before the paraffin lamp was developed, has continued to the present day, and there are still a few homes where it has not been replaced by electricity, even in advanced European countries. Beside me as I write this in 1977 lies the current edition of the local weekly newspaper *The Bucks Free Press*, open at the property pages. One cottage for sale in the centre of the small town of Great Missenden is advertised 'complete with gas lighting'. The advertisement adds: 'A grant should be available for installation of electricity.' Who knows, perhaps the buyers will prefer the soft, reassuring hiss of burning gas mantles which many people may recall nostalgically from their childhood days—the sound for me is forever linked in my mind with wonderful holidays spent in Scotland at my uncle's manse in a Tweedside village where most homes were still lit in this way. I have fond memories, too, of going upstairs to bed by candlelight, also in Scotland, at the home of my great aunt at New Abbey in Kirkcudbrightshire. Her home had electric lighting downstairs, but none upstairs.

Perhaps similar recollections of the happy past have made some people return to using gas light in the home. I know of one house in Fulham, London, where the owner has gas lighting throughout and can turn all the lights on by a simple switch near his front door. Each gas lamp has a pilot light.

Fortunately for such enthusiasts, gas mantles and spare parts are still produced. And even if you personally feel you can't do without electric light, wouldn't a few gas lamps in the home today be an added insurance against power failures of the sort that plunged New York into darkness a few years ago? It may be difficult, but it is not impossible to buy old fittings and shades that have not been converted to electricity.

Many of the old gas lamps were very attractive, particularly the table lamps with opaque white glass shades on which designs were painted in colour. Gas lamps were very similar to oil lamps in design, except that after 1905 the globes and shades were inverted. An interesting type of gas lighting was the water slide chandelier, which was suspended from the ceiling and could be raised or lowered as required. It worked on a telescopic principle, with one tube sliding inside another, and had a water seal to prevent gas from escaping. The outer tube, which supported the gas brackets, was counter-balanced by weights and pulleys.

Some collectors like to have one or two old gas street lamps, perhaps for the outside of the home, or for the garden—the iron-framed lantern-like lamps that remind us of the old lamplighters, for example, or later copper or brass mounted lamps with glass globes. Even some old electric street lights, especially the standard type, are worthy of being rescued from the scrapyard, and can add a touch of distinction to any garden.

An unusually stylish
Art Nouveau bronze
lamp by the Czech
J. Kratina. A gilt-
bronze semi-nude
figure of a girl supports
a painted glass panel
of a water landscape.
1900–1910. Fitted for
electricity. *Photo:
Sotheby's, London*

ELECTRICITY: THE RIVALS

The possibility that electricity might be utilised for lighting was fully recognised at the start of the nineteenth century, and there were demonstrations of arc lighting in the streets of Paris in the 1840s. But arc lights were of little practical use except in wide open spaces, and it was not until the filament lamp was developed that it became possible to use electricity for domestic lighting.

There has always been intense controversy between the British and the Americans over who was the first to demonstrate successfully a practical filament lamp. Was it Joseph Swan, of Newcastle upon Tyne, England, or was it that genius Thomas Edison of New York?

And do I detect a touch of jealousy, or perhaps lip-curling disbelief that a publicity-grabbing Yank could really go on besting European scientists, in this excerpt from a contemporary book, *Electric Light* by C. W. Urquhart, in 1880?

Much interest has been taken in the sensational and often absurd announcements concerning the apparatus in course of perfection by Mr T. A. Edison, of Menlo Park, New York. This inventor is well-known by his talking phonograph and telephones, and it was in some quarters thought that when he had set himself to the task of inventing an efficient subdivision of the electric light circuit something in all probability would be done. Unfortunately, however, as far as can be learned up to this date the attempts have proved almost complete failures . . .

The latest outcome of Mr Edison's praiseworthy labours to obtain a constant burner by electric agency, is a small lamp in the form of a glass globe, exhausted of air, and containing in the electric circuit a horseshoe shaped strip of carbonised cardboard . . . It is claimed that a lamp may be produced at an outlay of 25 cents. A number of these lamps were seen burning in the

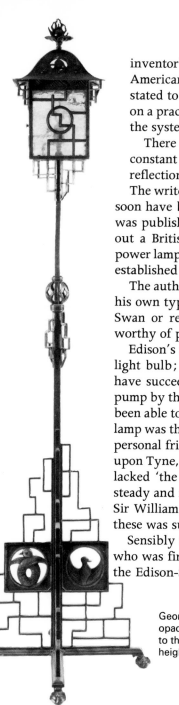

inventor's laboratory by correspondents of the press, English and American, during the month of December, 1879. The result is stated to be so satisfactory that Mr Edison intends to illuminate, on a practical scale, the village of Menlo Park, and then to extend the system to New York.

There is little probability, however, that this lamp will prove constant . . . We may, indeed, rest assured that, upon further reflection, Mr Edison will abandon this imperfect burner.

The writer of this rather condescending piece of sour grapes must soon have been feeling pretty silly. In the very year that the book was published, 1880, came the news that Edison—who had taken out a British patent the year before—had produced a 16-candle power lamp with carbonised bamboo filaments. And by 1882 he had established the promised electricity supply for New York.

The author Urquhart was himself an inventor and had developed his own type of arc light, but he had either never heard of Joseph Swan or regarded the research he was conducting as not being worthy of placing on record.

Edison's first successful bulb was pear shaped, like the modern light bulb; Swan's was more like a cucumber. But neither would have succeeded if it had not been for the invention of a vacuum pump by the German scientist Herman Springel, and if they had not been able to call on the help of expert glass blowers. Swan's electric lamp was the first actually to be used in a private house—that of his personal friend Sir William Armstrong at Cragside, near Newcastle upon Tyne, in December 1880. Sir William announced that the light lacked 'the disagreeable attributes of the arc light. It is perfectly steady and noiseless. It is free from harsh glare and dark shadows.' Sir William had 45 lamps installed in his home and the power for these was supplied by a water turbine generator.

Sensibly the two rivals decided to abandon their squabble about who was first, and pooled their knowledge and expertise, forming the Edison-Swan Electric Company in Britain in 1883. There were

Geometric Art Nouveau standard lamp in copper. The shade is formed of opaque glass panels with geometric banding. The four stepped supports to the adjustable centre column enclose plaques of birds. Maximum height is 6 feet. Late 19th century. *Photo: Sotheby's, London*

Left: A fine adjustable desk lamp, Edwardian. *Collection: Fred and Joan Crickard*

Right: A simple brass Edwardian desk lamp.

rapid developments in electric lighting, but Swan's carbon filament made of squirted cellulose remained standard until the end of century.

Yet it was still a very long time before electricity replaced oil lamps and gas, which received a tremendous boost when the incandescent gas mantle was introduced in the 1880s. And even homes equipped with gas or electricity found that oil lamps and candles remained necessary as supplementary lighting. Often there was a piped supply of gas only to the ground floor of a house, so that oil lamps and candles were required for all lighting on the floors above. Equally, many of the wealthy people who enjoyed the brilliance of the new-fangled electric light had to have their own generators. These generators were subject to breakdown and were extremely noisy, so that it was desirable to have them some distance from the house if the full benefit of the 'noiselessness' of electric light

Hand-carved walnut ceiling lamp with simulated candle holders for the light bulbs. Probably Edwardian. *Collection: George and Grace Oakley*

was to be received; and they were not always powerful enough to maintain a reasonably satisfactory degree of lighting for every room in the house if most of the lights were switched on at the same time. So, once again, stand-by oil lamps and candles were essential—and perhaps remained the only light supplied for the servants' rooms. It is not surprising to find that a London store catalogue, not long before the first European war, devotes six pages to gas lamps and fittings, ten to electrical fittings, nineteen to oil lamps, and one and a half pages to candle lamps. Collectors should thus be warned that many of the 'Victorian' oil lamps offered in antique shops and collectors' markets may in fact be of a much later date.

When studying old catalogues it is striking how little difference the coming of electric lighting at first made to the shapes of lamps and light fittings. The hanging lamps and standard lamps for oil, gas and electricity remained remarkably similar, and many of the shades were interchangeable. Electric lamps of the 1890s and early 1900s are nevertheless very desirable items today.

104

Many of these late Victorian and early Edwardian electric light fittings are now reappearing in modern homes. Apart from the ceiling and standard lamps, examples of the table lamps and brass desk lamps are worthy of the collector's attention. Early twentieth century bicycle and automobile electric lamps are now in the category of collectables, and in the past few years some Americans have started to collect old Christmas tree lamps, and—as usually happens when the American collector finds new directions for his hobby—the European collector will eventually follow.

It is logical, however, that the fad for collecting Christmas tree lamps should start in the United States. The very first electrically lit Christmas tree appeared in the New York City home of Edward H. Johnson, a friend of Edison. The lights were miniature incandescent lamps, miniature replicas of Edison's pear-shaped lamps. Three years later sets of this type of Christmas lamp were offered for sale to the American public. Some very attractive sets were issued during

Below left: Attractive table lamp with painted plaster figure of a Japanese lady and a bamboo shade. Circa 1930. *Collection: George and Grace Oakley*

Below right: Table lamp with a base formed of porcelain group of dancing cherubs. Crossed swords mark. *Collection: Joan and Fred Crickard*

the first half of the century, notably by the General Electric Company in America and the Kremenetzky Electric Company of Vienna. These lamps were all brightly coloured and many were in human or animal shapes—Father Christmas, inevitably, being a feature of most sets. The Eveready Mazda set for 1910 included lamps shaped like a clown, a lion, a dog, a cat, a policeman, a monkey, a Dutch girl, a trumpeter girl, a parrot, a robin, and various fruits. Collectors like to find these lamps still in their attractively decorated wooden boxes.

Left: Mushroom shape cut-glass table lamp from the 1920s. *Collection: Author*

Centre: Continental bisque figure, 19th century, converted into a table lamp. *Collection: Gwen Hughes*

Right: Porcelain lady forms the base of a 1930s electric table lamp. *Collection: Mrs Henry Aaronson*

SEARCH FOR SAFETY

Mr Spedding, the colliery manager who was nearly a hundred years ahead of his time with his scheme to provide gas lighting for the town of Whitehaven, has another claim to fame in the history of lighting. He was the first man to tackle the problem of providing safe illumination in coal mines.

Until Spedding introduced his spark mill about 1730, the only illumination possible in mines had been by candle or oil lamp, which were quite safe for the Romans and later miners who went digging underground for metal ores, but not at all suitable for the men who first went mining for coal in tunnels where explosive fire damp caused many accidents and deaths.

Why sparks? Surely they were dangerous, too, in places where fire damp was present? Sir James Lowther was one man who was confident that spark mills were safe, and he wrote in a paper presented to the Royal Society in 1734:

This sort of vapour or damp air will not take fire except by flame; sparks do not affect it, and for that reason it is frequent to use flint and steel in places affected by this sort of damp, which will give a glimmering light that is a great help to the workmen.

Not all the men who worked in the eighteenth and nineteenth century coal mines trusted declarations of this sort by those who were unlikely to put their claims to the test by going underground in dangerous conditions themselves. In fact, many of the miners preferred to work in darkness rather than by the faint light provided by Spedding's spark mill, which nevertheless became more or less standard equipment in European coal mines until the early part of the nineteenth century. The sparks were produced by holding a flint against a rotating iron wheel, which had to be kept turning throughout the long working day. It was a frustrating and repetitive task that was usually performed by young boys. The

Flint mill for use in coal mines in the 18th and early 19th centuries. The sparks gave a glimmering light, but their supposed safety value was minimal.
Photo: Crown copyright, Science Museum, London

spark mills were costly and required a lot of maintenance: it was a full-time job for one man to keep six spark mills in good condition. There is no doubt that they were a little safer than naked flame lamps, and they did give some warning of the danger of explosion, as the sparks tended to appear larger and shine more brightly when damp was present. They failed to save Mr Spedding's life, however: he was killed in a mine explosion in 1765.

It was not until 1813 that anyone came up with a better way of providing illumination in coal mines. In that year Dr William Reid Clanny designed a new safety lamp which had an air-tight chamber for the burner. Air for combustion was pumped into it with a bellows. There were water seals both for the air from the bellows and for the exhaust gases, so that all the air entering or leaving the lamp passed through the water. The idea was that the water would cool the gases and reduce the risk of explosion. The Clanny lamp was the first reasonably safe mine lamp, but it was a clumsy, cumbersome contrivance, and a man was needed to work full-time operating the bellows. It never came into general use.

The man who made the real breakthrough was Sir Humphry Davy, with his lamps enclosed by gauze. It is possible that he may have got the basic idea for his lamps from the gauze-protected lanterns which had been in use in barns and granaries where inflammable chaff and dust was present in the air. The gauze prevented the chaff from coming into contact with the flame and being ignited. There was no way in which a gauze screen could guarantee that the oil lamp flame would not come into contact with gases outside the screen but Davy reasoned that the metal mesh he used would cool down the flame before it came into contact with any possible fire damp, which explodes at certain temperatures but will extinguish a flame that is below these temperatures. The gauze of the Davy lamp gave warning of the presence of concentrations of fire damp by glowing a dull red in certain conditions.

After experimenting with glass and metal tubes, Davy devised a lamp in which the air entered through small tubes with wire-covered apertures below the flame, and the flame was protected by a wire gauze cylinder. Davy at first chose a gauze with 6,400 apertures per square inch, but eventually after further experiments it was realised that such a fine mesh was erring on the side of caution and a mesh of only 784 apertures per square inch was adopted as standard. The fact that the flame was totally unprotected from draughts was unsatisfactory, however, as sudden gusts of air could fan the flame and force it through the cooling gauze at a temperature that could ignite fire damp. So one of the first improvements, introduced by Davy himself, was to protect the flame from draughts by placing shields in front of the gauze.

Until 1839 the gauze screen was the full depth of the safety lamp. Then Dr Clanny improved the illuminating power by surrounding the flame itself with a glass cylinder and employing gauze mesh only on the upper section of the lamp. In later Clanny lamps the upper gauze was protected by a metal bonnet which made it even safer if there were sudden gusts of air. Improvements by other

The Davy lamp as it progressed. *Photo: Crown copyright, Science Museum, London*

people included the provision of a chimney or chimneys to reduce a tendency to throw off smoke. Further improvements to the Clanny lamp were made by the Frenchman Marsaut in the 1880s. In Marsaut's lamp two conical gauze caps were situated over the flame, one more sharply pointed than the other, and a bonnet enclosed both of them. The air entered by holes in the bottom of the lamp, just above the glass section, and the waste gases after combustion left through holes in the bonnet above the gauze cones.

Because of their usefulness in detecting the presence of gas, the

110

Miner's lamp, early 20th century, with glass sleeve and ventilation holes under the cap.

Davy and Clanny type of safety lamps continued to be used in mines long after it was possible to have electric lamps. Even when it became standard practice for the men at the coalface to have electric lamps attached to their caps so that both hands were left free for hewing and shovelling, the safety lamps continued to be used by examiners, firemen and deputies.

Electric hand lamps with bodies made of wood were being used for some purposes underground in Glasgow and Nottingham from as early as 1883, and a couple of examples of this type of lamp could form the basis of a collection of wooden battery hand lamps. But the old safety oil lamp, with its gleaming brass or brass and steel body is certain to remain a favourite among collectors. There were many variations on the basic lamp, apart from the developments I have already mentioned, and there is an added point of interest, evocative of the industrial past, in the name plates of the manufacturers or suppliers of the lamps in places where the Industrial Revolution was born—Wigan, Leigh, Nottingham, Glasgow, Gateshead on Tyne, for example.

To improve on a collection of mine lamps from the Humphry

Davy period onwards, it would be satisfying to have also a few of the earlier types of lamp that were used in mines. The Romans in their metal ore mines used spoon-shaped oil lamps made of lead with a straight stem which could be used either for carrying the lamp or for sticking it into the wall of the mine so that both hands were free for work. One type of closed oil lamp popular in British mines before the eighteenth century was a small one of coffee-pot shape with a protruding spout, a hinged lid and a hook to enable it to be hung from a miner's belt. Another lamp that was popular in parts of continental Europe had a flat closed reservoir with an iron loop for carrying, and a long, hooked rod by which it could be suspended. In German mines open-fronted wooden lanterns for either oil lamps or candles were used until the nineteenth century!

Miner's electric safety lamps, in use as early as 1883. *Photo: Crown copyright, Science Museum, London*

THE BRILLIANCE OF TIFFANY

The coming of the electrical era coincided with that vital surging artistic movement called Art Nouveau. You either love it or you hate it, but you can never deny the originality and craftsmanship of the many fine artists and sculptors who embraced it. And there was one man, a leader of the movement, who took the brilliant glaring light of electricity and used it to create a new beauty of colour and line with his magnificent lamps made of metal and glass—the American Louis Comfort Tiffany.

He developed a completely new iridescent stained glass in a whole range of peacock colours that proved to be the perfect medium for diffusing and softening the harshness of electric light. A lamp is more than a number of pieces of coloured glass, however, and Tiffany's metal frames and bases in typically sinuous and sensuous lines completed an integral whole that was pure Art Nouveau. Europeans sometimes claim that he was the only American who understood what the movement was aiming for.

Tiffany's lamps, like all his other work in glass, were craftsman-made luxury items and were expensive in their own time—100 dollars each for the popular standard lamps, for example. Yet such was their appeal and renown that no well-off American who claimed to live in any sort of style could exist without owning at least one genuine Tiffany lamp. And those among the aristocracy and nouveau riche in Europe who professed to appreciate the attractions of Art Nouveau bought Tiffany lamps, vases and other items of art glass in quite considerable quantities from the shop of Samuel Bing in Paris, La Maison de l'Art Nouveau, which gave its name to the movement.

If Tiffany *was* unique as an American who understood Art Nouveau, it was probably due to the fact that he spent ten years in Europe right at the period when the movement was reaching its full

A variant on Tiffany's Dragonfly theme: a magnificent lamp.

development, and mixed with most of the leading lights of the artistic world, including Whistler, Rossetti and Oscar Wilde.

Louis Tiffany was the son of Charles Tiffany, the New York jeweller, but he had no inclinations to go into the family business. Instead, he decided that he wanted to be a painter, and sailed for Europe to study under George Innes and Samuel Coleman. Thus

Dragonfly lamp. It has a mottled pale green shade in bronze-patinated leading, set with green glass droplet jewels. The dragonflies form the rim, with their bodies and wings in shades of blue, green and turquoise glass. The elaborate bronze base is stamped *Tiffany Studios New York 550* underneath. *Photo: Sotheby's, London*

Lily lamp from Tiffany Studios. The gold lustre shades are modelled as lily flowers, and even though two of the seven original shades are missing this would still be an expensive lamp for the collector. It brought £1350 (2500 dollars) at Phillips, London, in 1976.

began the most formative years of the young Tiffany's life in which he encountered and absorbed many new and strange ideas and influences. He patronised Liberty's Oriental Warehouse in London and was impressed by the Middle-eastern decorative objects which were then in vogue. It is almost certain also that he visited the Victoria and Albert Museum in Kensington and saw the wonderful display of iridescent glass on show in the early Syrian and Roman collections.

Eventually the life of a young American-about-Europe who didn't need to worry too much about where the next buck would come from came to an end, as all good things must, and he returned to New York to set about the serious business of making his own living. Along with Coleman and Candance Wheeler he set up an interior design firm which he called Louis C. Tiffany and Associated Artists in 1875, when he was 27. No doubt family connections helped the firm in gaining commissions from wealthy Americans. But there is no doubt also that the firm's work was greatly appreciated by the

Left: A Tiffany lamp in the simple style. *Photo: Sotheby's, London*

Right: Typical Tiffany: this elegant table lamp has a domed shade with a band of scrolling pate ochre foliage on a green ground with bands of geometric panels. *Photo: Christie's, London*

owners of the luxurious homes who commissioned it, and in 1882 Tiffany and his colleagues were busy redecorating the White House. Their work at this time was mainly concerned with textiles and furnishings, but Tiffany was also experimenting with glass. The interiors he designed at this time brought a touch of oriental splendour to New York and Washington mansions, not least with the leaded glass panes which Tiffany used to create ornamental designs in stained glass windows.

Some researchers believe that Tiffany's interest in blown glass stemmed from the need to make use of the surplus pieces of glass left over from the windows the company made and installed. Other glassmakers, notably Webb at Stourbridge in England, had already experimented with the manufacture of iridescent glass, and Hungarian manufacturers had shown examples at the Vienna World Exhibition in 1873. To help in his experiments Tiffany employed some master craftsmen. One was the Venetian glassblower Andrea Boldini and another the Englishman Arthur Nash, who had worked at Stourbridge under Webb and already understood some of the techniques required for introducing iridescence into glass. It has been said that Nash was such a skilled glassblower and could control the flowing mass of glass so expertly, that he could introduce colour at will.

Tiffany's technique for introducing colour into the glass came to be known as *favrile* ('by hand'), and as early as 1880 Tiffany had applied for a patent for Favrile glass. The foundation glass, after reheating, was sprayed with a vapourised solution of salts of iron or tin. Then, after the basic shape of the piece had been formed, but while it was still malleable, it was reheated and sprayed with metallic vapours which were absorbed by the molten glass and formed layers of reflecting colour when the object had cooled and set. A copper vapour spray could give colours ranging from a greenish blue to a rich ruby, according to the conditions in the furnace, which the glassmakers learned to judge by experience. Cobalt vapour gave a range of blue shades, but if mixed with manganese it produced a dense black.

The Favrile type of coloured glass was totally different from the old stained glass which had been used in Europe for centuries. This was normally clear glass with the colour applied to the surface only,

Left: Art Deco wrought-iron and glass table lamp with two bell shades in orange glass shading to purple. The shades are marked *Muller Fres Luneville.* Photo: *Sotheby's, London*

Right: Tiffany Studios oil lamp. Mottled pale green glass with a band of ivy leaves in orange and green. 20 inches high. *Photo: Christies, London*

and Tiffany wrote:

> By the aid of studies in chemistry and through years of experiments, I have found the means to avoid the use of paints, etching or burning or otherwise treating the surface of the glass so that it is now possible to produce figures in glass of which even the finest flesh tones are not superficially treated—built up of what I call 'genuine glass' because there are no tricks of the glassmaker needed to express flesh.

These early experiments by Tiffany were carried out at the Heidt glassworks in Brooklyn. Then in the late 1880s he changed his company's name to the Tiffany Glass and Decorating Company and opened the Tiffany furnaces at Corona, Long Island. A very high standard of craftsmanship was demanded from all his workers, but Arthur Nash seems to have considered himself the true maestro of Tiffany glass—Nash's family later claimed that it was he who had carried out all the really important development work on Favrile glass. Robert Koch, author of *Louis C. Tiffany, Rebel In Glass,* on the other hand has written that after interviewing surviving glass workers from the Corona furnaces it was his opinion that 'Arthur J. Nash was not a master glassblower, and the credit for the unique quality of Tiffany's Favrile glass should be given to Thomas Manderson, Tiffany's first gaffer.' Whatever the truth of this controversy, there is no doubt that Tiffany himself, the true guiding genius of the whole operation, valued Nash's contribution highly; so highly that Nash was the only man he employed who was allowed to sign his own work.

Coleman and Wheeler, Tiffany's original partners, did not share

A splendid Galle lamp.
Photo: Sotheby's, London

his enthusiasm for experimentation with glass, and went their own individual ways. Meanwhile in France Emil Galle was conducting similar experiments with glass. He was the son of a producer and retailer of decorative glassware in Nancy, and when his father died in 1874, Emil, then 28, become head of the family firm. In the next 30 years, until he died of leukemia in 1904, Emil Galle built up the small local business into what was probably the largest factory in Europe manufacturing luxury glassware.

For the first ten years Galle produced mainly transparent glass with either a clear or slightly tinted body, decorated with enamel paints. At this time he was strongly influenced by Eastern and Renaissance models and produced, among other things, some fine copies of Islamic mosque lamps.

By 1884 he had abandoned his belief that glass should always be absolutely transparent. Like Tiffany he experimented with metallic oxides and produced glass that seemed to have flights of bubbles or explosions of colour trapped in the body. Unlike Tiffany, however, he used the engraver's wheel to add decoration, and in 1889 he showed his first cameo glass vases. These had one or more overlays which were cut back so that the pattern stood out in relief against a background of a different colour. At first all Galle's glass was hand-cut, but later mass production was adopted and acid was used for the cutting, so that a very large proportion of the cameo glass that bears Galle's name is not of the same fine quality as his early work. Nevertheless, glass vases and lamps using the acid-etching technique bring high prices at auction, as do those produced by the Daum brothers, whose cameo glass could also be excellent.

Some of the best work by Galle, however, employed the *marquetrie-sur-verre* technique. For this he applied semi-molten glass to the body of the vase to be decorated while it was still soft and pliable, rolled the additional glass flat with the surface, then completed the decoration with some hand carving.

All the leading arbiters of design and taste in Europe were already familiar with Galle's innovations and fine work when they went to Paris to visit Samuel Bing's newly-opened Maison de l'Art Nouveau in 1895, but they had not seen any of Tiffany's glass before. The 20 pieces he shipped across the Atlantic specially for the opening caused a sensation, and made Tiffany's name in Europe. Thus

122

Examples of Galle's double overlay technique. *Photo: Christies, London*

encouraged, he appointed Bing his sole distributor in Europe and five years later changed his firm's name to Tiffany Studios. About the same time he established a department of metalwork to make the bases and mounts for his increasingly sought after lamps.

The designers of Tiffany lamps always gave them a continuous theme, the metal base and pillar being as important as the beautifully coloured sections of glass that made up the shade. Clara Driscoll, for instance, achieved a rare harmony between the verdigris bronze structure of her Dragonfly lamps and the greens, blues and mauves of the glass. Other designs were based on spiders' webs, water lilies and turtle shells. Perhaps the lamp most collectors covet, one which invariably reaches a very high price when an example is offered for sale, is the Wistaria lamp, which was designed by Mrs Curtis Freshel. But I rather suspect that Louis Tiffany himself would have chosen the Peacock lamps and vases if he had been asked to select the series of designs he personally preferred. He was certainly aware of the appropriateness of the proud peacock as a symbol for Tiffany's genius, as he demonstrated when he gave a party for some of his male friends and business associates in New York in 1914. A bevy of beautiful girls clad in classical costumes paraded live peacocks in front of the assembled guests; and the main dish set before them at the dining table was peacock. The occasion was sure confirmation, if it were needed, that Tiffany combined a shrewd, down-to-earth realism with an unusual and imaginative artistic flair.

It was this flair, combined with his genuine business sense, that made Louis C. Tiffany undoubtedly the most important of all the Art Nouveau makers of decorative glass. However desirable and attractive many of the European lamps made by people like Galle and the Daum brothers might be, it is always the Tiffany lamps that command the highest prices in the world's leading sale rooms. Unfortunately they are usually beyond the reach of all but the most affluent collectors.

For some two post-World War 1 generations all Art Nouveau was regarded as decadent and ugly, before it was rediscovered and taken to their hearts by the young people of the swinging 1960s. Most of it was discarded by the sons and daughters of the original owners, so

A bronze table lamp signed I. C. Saden. Early 20th century. *Photo: Bonham's, London*

124

125

there are almost certainly still some fine examples of Tiffany lamps lurking at the back of somebody's attic or junk room—each one a hidden treasure that could bring the finder a windfall large enough to buy a small house, or two or three automobiles.

Tiffany was much copied in his own time, both in America and in Europe, and while the copyists never quite achieved the same effect as Tiffany, many of their works are also worth collecting today. Most genuine Tiffany lamps, but not all, are marked 'Tiffany Studios' on the base. There have been many reproductions in recent years, so if you are offered any Tiffany lamp at what seems a bargain price, make sure you have it authenticated before you part with any money.

Not that reproductions are all bad and undesirable. Few people can afford the really splendid old Tiffany lamps, and some modern manufacturers have captured the style of the period quite well, even if they cannot fully reproduce the iridescence of the old glass. Perhaps the best Tiffany-style lamps of today are produced in London by Christopher Wray, who has a Tiffany shop in Kings Road, Chelsea, and another in Paris. His lamps are hand-made in his own workshops and the glass panes he uses are produced by the same process that Tiffany initiated. Wray's admiration for Tiffany may stem from the fact that they have similar traits of artistic flair and business drive. Wray was a repertory and television actor before his hobby became his business, and he set up as a dealer in old lamps and a manufacturer of quality reproductions. Straight copies of the old style were not enough to satisfy his artistic temperament, so he also makes lamps of his own design. His tall 'tree' lamps particularly are an extension of Tiffany's style, the metal bases and stems being intricately hand-worked. Craftsman-made items like these could well become the collectables of the future.

Before leaving the subject of Tiffany I should mention that not all the lamps made in his workshops were electric lamps. Particularly in the early years, there were many very fine oil lamps with Favrile glass shades, which also bring high prices. They suffer by comparison with electric lamps, not because of any inferiority of workmanship, but because the much fainter light from the burning wick of an oil lamp does not satisfactorily demonstrate the remarkable qualities of the coloured glass. Nor, unfortunately, do photographs, even coloured ones.

126

AFTER ART DECO: WHAT NEXT?

People buy old lamps for a variety of reasons. Probably the most usual reason is that they want to have lighting that is contemporary with the style of furnishing in their homes. So anyone whose taste is for Georgian or Victorian furniture will have some old oil lamps, probably converted to electricity for convenience. Others who have oak furniture from earlier periods may have only simple, discreet electric fittings, and dim their lamps when there are guests so that they can dine by candlelight from an old oak refectory table. I know of a builder in England who insisted on having only the finest French-style furnishings in the splendid home he was building for himself, and purchased at considerable expense a magnificent chandelier, converted for electricity, from a French château. He had it shipped across the Channel, but when it was delivered at his home there was no position he could install it in, because from top to bottom it was deeper than the height of any of his rooms. No problem—at least for a determined builder. He had his men dig a well in the floor to make room for his treasure, and now the guests can inspect and admire the chandelier as they walk round it.

Other people collect lamps because they have a special personal significance, perhaps bringing to mind some event from the past. I saw two splendid early Art Deco lamps in a house in Oxfordshire, which had originally been fittings in the Cunard transatlantic liner *Berengaria* between the wars. The first time Mr Ken Weightman, who now owns them, saw the lamps was when as a young boy he and his family sat down to dinner in the dining room of the *Berengaria* moored in New York harbour in 1938. The family were about to return to England from Canada where the father, an executive in an insurance company, had been working. They were due to sail early next morning, and after the meal, during which they all admired the elegant lamps on the tables, they went to their suite and settled in for

Left: Table lamp with straight, simple lines of the early Art Deco period. Rescued from the transatlantic liner *Berengaria* after it was broken up. *Collection: Ken Weightman*

Right: Cubist-style table lamp with frosted glass panels in a silvered metal frame with four squares of silvered metal above, around a central pierced ventilation shaft. Square hardwood base, the underside stamped *Lucien Lelong. Photo: Sotheby's, London*

the night. Between two and three in the morning there was a loud hammering on the door and Ken opened it to be told by a member of the crew that the ship was on fire and they must evacuate it. He woke his sister, who at first refused to believe him, thinking that his story was just a mischievous prank. They all escaped safely but the liner was extensively damaged. Disaster for the steamship company brought a full week's holiday in New York at Cunard's expense, and Mrs Weightman in particular had a great time, going to a different show every night. At the end of the week they all sailed for home in the *Queen Mary*.

The *Berengaria* was taken back to England and never made another passenger voyage. But the family all remembered the lamps they had seen in the dining room and were delighted when Ken's father bought two of them at an auction sale organised by the insurers. The lamps had apparently been the cause of the disaster: during the 1914–18 war the *Berengaria* had been used as a troopship and was completely refitted afterwards, but not all the electrical wiring had been renewed and it was a fault in the wiring to the table lamps that started the fire. That is a point for collectors of old electrical lamps to note: make sure that any wiring is safe before you use them.

It is just such a wish as Ken Weightman's, to have a link with the past, to be able to take a nostalgic look over the shoulder, that makes the collector what he is. And his father made a shrewd buy, too. Much of the nostalgia today is for that period between the two Great

An Austrian table lamp, with a crescent shaped bronze stem spreading to form a circular support for the yellow iridescent glass shade, with elaborate decoration in pale blue and gold lustre. The bronze base is by Gustav Gurschner, and the glass shade is probably by Loetz. *Photo: Sotheby's, London*

 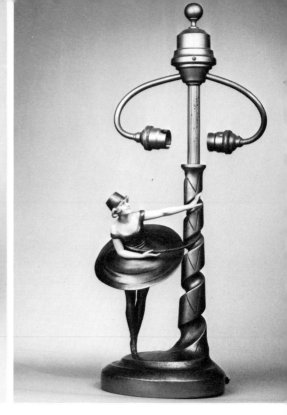

Wars when the *Berengaria's* lamps were made: the era of prohibition, *The Great Gatsby*, *The Ziegfeld Follies*, the platinum blondes and the style-setting smart new ocean liners fitted and furnished exclusively in the with-it new fashion called Art Deco.

There were two major influences from which Art Deco blossomed—one from the very ancient world and the other ultra-modern. The ancient, three-thousand-year-old influence was that of King Tutankhamen whose tomb was opened by Howard Carter in November 1922; and the ultra-modern one was that of the great cubist painters such as Picasso, Braque and Lèger.

So there was something of a conflict in Art Deco. On the one hand there were the craftsmen and artists who wanted their work to represent the soul of the new machine age; on the other those of a more romantic nature who avoided coldly clinical and geometric decoration in black and white and chrome. They were not so eager to tackle the realities and harshness of modern life head-on and preferred a naturalistic, colourful approach. But one thing all these

Right: Rare and unusual French bronze and cameo glass lamp. The domed shade is cameo cut with a view of the Pyramids, the Sphinx and figures in the desert beneath the moon, in shades of brown on a deep cream ground. The shade is signed *Muller Freres, Luneville,* and the bronze tree trunk support with a lioness and cubs is signed *L. Carvi.* Circa 1930. *Photo: Phillips, London*

Below: A rare pate de verre table lamp by G. Argy-Rousseau. *Photo: Christies, London*

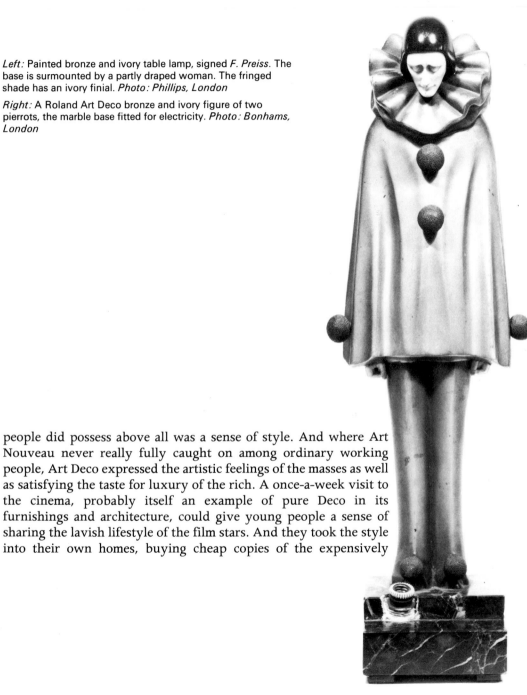

Left: Painted bronze and ivory table lamp, signed *F. Preiss*. The base is surmounted by a partly draped woman. The fringed shade has an ivory finial. *Photo: Phillips, London*

Right: A Roland Art Deco bronze and ivory figure of two pierrots, the marble base fitted for electricity. *Photo: Bonhams, London*

people did possess above all was a sense of style. And where Art Nouveau never really fully caught on among ordinary working people, Art Deco expressed the artistic feelings of the masses as well as satisfying the taste for luxury of the rich. A once-a-week visit to the cinema, probably itself an example of pure Deco in its furnishings and architecture, could give young people a sense of sharing the lavish lifestyle of the film stars. And they took the style into their own homes, buying cheap copies of the expensively

The home was often a square place in the 1920s, right down to the electric lamps.

produced statuettes and lamps and furniture that they saw in photographs in magazines, or on the cinema screen. The materials used might be plastic instead of ivory, or spelter instead of bronze, and the workmanship not all it might be, but the style was still unmistakable.

Most of the lamps produced for the luxury market, made by men such as Lalique, the Daum Brothers, Preiss and Chiparus, command high prices in the auction rooms. They went out of fashion so recently, however, that there are probably still many examples lying

134

Lemon squeezer? No, this is just an extravagant example of Art Deco taken to the extreme.

in private houses unrecognised as the valuable commodities they are.

Most of the inspiration for Art Deco came from France. And the greatest exponent of the style in glass was undoubtedly Réné Lalique, who produced articles moulded in his familiar frosted or milky blue glass in huge quantities. He made some really exceptional figures and lamps that were not mass produced. The fact that his production was so great means that all collectors have a chance of finding a nice piece of Lalique to buy. He made lamps in various

Lalique glass. The shallow inverted conical shade is supported above a knob moulded with stylised roses, extending into the trumpet base. The base and shade are in frosted glass with traces of pink staining. Signed *R. Lalique*. *Photo: Sotheby's, London*

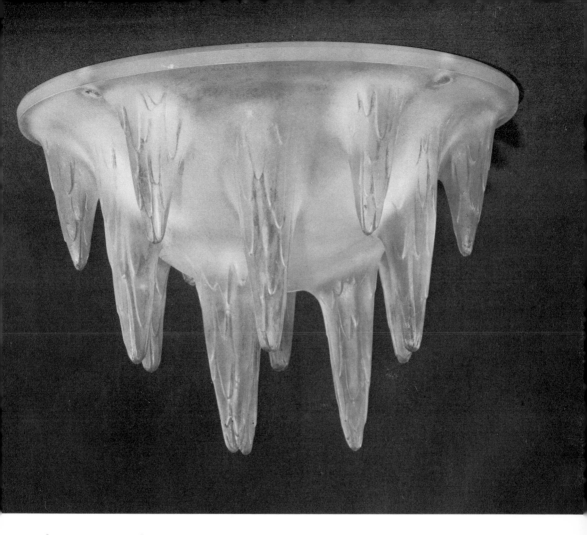

designs, among the most attractive being tall standard lamps with chrome stems supporting trumpet- or saucer-shaped bowls. All pieces of Lalique's glass bear his name, either engraved in handscript or moulded in capitals. Any item that carries the initial R. with the name Lalique was made before 1945, the year of his death. His style was aped by others, such as Muller, Hunebelle and Sabino, and these are also collectable examples of Art Deco.

A word that frequently crops up when people are discussing Art Deco is 'chryselephantine' which, according to my dictionary means 'made of gold and ivory'. But the so-called chryselephantine

Unusual Lalique ceiling shade in frosted glass, moulded with stalactites, with traces of red staining. *Photo: Sotheby's, London*

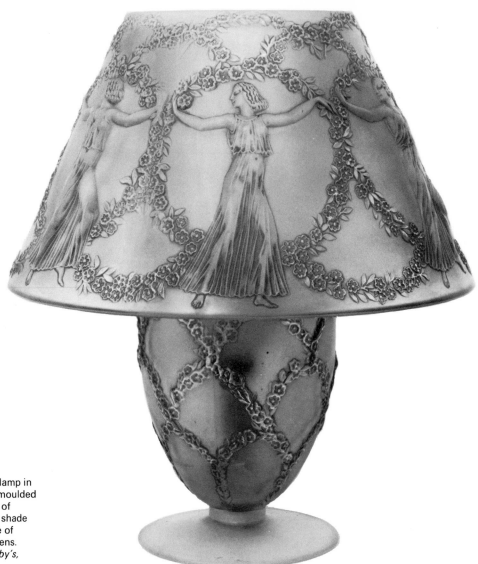

Lalique glass lamp in
frosted glass moulded
with a design of
garlands. The shade
carries a frieze of
dancing maidens.
*Photo: Sotheby's,
London*

sculptures of the 1920s and 30s, often incorporated in electric table
lamps with appropriate shades, employed bronze in place of gold. It
was a period when vast quantities of ivory were available from the
Belgian colonies in Africa, and the Belgian Government encouraged

Below: Daum Lakescape cameo glass lamp. The hemispherical shade in mottled yellow/green glass over laid in black is etched with fishing boats. The stem is etched with seaweed fronds. The shade is signed *Daum Nancy. Photo: Sotheby's, London*

Right: Muller Freres cameo glass lamp. Green glass body with internal streaks of blue, overlaid in deep red, blue and purple glass, and etched with design of wild anemones. *Photo: Sotheby's, London*

Bronze and ivory dancing girl dressed in a red and gold harlequin suit, holding a lantern in each outstretched hand. The mottled black and brown marble base is engraved with the mark *Bouraine*. 1920s.

A large etched glass ceiling lamp, with a broad domed shade supported from a slender stem and small domed ceiling plate. Pale yellow glass deeply acid etched and decorated with scatted gold foil inclusions. Marked *Daum, Nancy, France.* Circa 1935. 18 inches wide. *Photo: Sotheby's, London*

sculptors and others to make use of the material. The figures, usually females either nude or scantily dressed (eroticism has always been one of the greatest inspirations for artists and always will be), stand on marble or onyx bases. These have become quite expensive to collect for a number of reasons, partly because ivory is now scarce, partly because of the brilliant craftsmanship of the sculptors, and partly because the 1920s are in fashion again.

The greatest sculptors in the new type of chryselephantine were Frederick Preiss and Demetre Chiparus. Preiss was a master of the nude figury in ivory, attending to detail in hands and faces with meticulous precision. His figures are often subtly tinted and he had a talent for capturing the spirit of movement. Many of his athletic leaping figures have an exciting lifelike quality, but some people see a sinister influence in his work. His semi-nude girl athletes have a Germanic look and are believed to represent the ideal young Nazi of the 1930s.

The work of Chiparus, a Rumanian who settled in France, may not be so precise as that of Preiss, but his figures express a fine feeling of opulence. They are often gaudily gilded and stand on ponderous variegated marble bases. He took inspiration almost equally from

Glass table lamp of the 1930s. The conical shade is supported on three small arms above a spherical base. Frosted glass enamelled with bands of blue, shading to burgundy.
Photo: Sotheby's, London

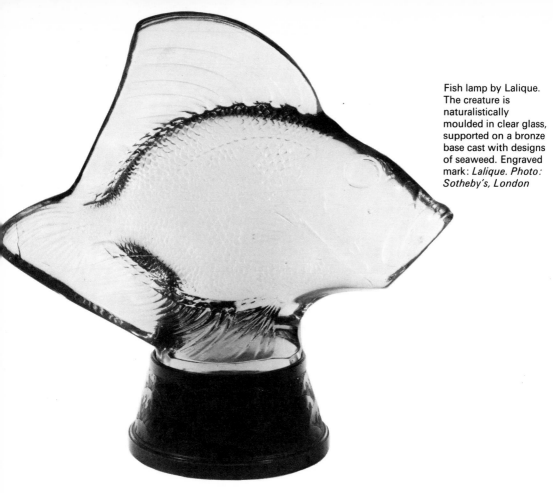

theatrical and Hollywood spectaculars, and the splendours of
ancient Egypt as revealed after the opening of Tutankhamen's tomb.
He modelled young women in pleated skirts and gave them Egyptian
head-dresses. His ivory slave girls wore jewelled tops and sandals,
and ornamented armbands and necklaces.

All Chiparus's chryselephantine figures and lamps sold well, and
he was businesslike enough to cash in by reproducing his designs in
less costly materials for the mass market. Other names to look out for
on bronze and ivory sculptures include Bruno Zavh, Kelety, Paul
Phillippe, Camus, Lorenzl and Colinet.

Cheaper copies of the expensive Art Deco lamps made by the great
craftsmen are often very attractive, and there is plenty of scope for

Only a gentle glimmer came from this lamp, circa 1940, but it was enough to guide a policeman or air raid warden through darkened streets in wartime Britain.

the collector to find electric lamps at almost give-away prices at the lower end of the market. The lower end of the market invariably seems within a few years to become the upper end, as the supply of items for the new collectors to buy diminishes, so if you choose carefully, with an eye for good design, the lamps you buy are almost certain to increase in value. I do not suggest, on the other hand, that investment should ever be your first or only consideration. If you always buy lamps that you like and can live with happily, your hard-earned money will never have been wasted.

And what will be the next generation of collectable lamps? Already there is an interest in wartime lamps made for use in the blackout, such as the British Air Raid Warden's lamp that cast what little illumination it gave downwards so that no enemy air crew looking for signs of habitation could see their light. Perhaps even the plastic lamps of the 1950s, now scorned as out of date, will seize the imagination of collectors yet unborn.

144